S@NG FOR
DEMETER

for David

S(A)NG FOR
DEMETER

RICHARD KEMBLE

All Best Wishes

Richard Kemble

9/8/24

Matador
9 Priory Business Park,
Wistow Road, Kibworth Beauchamp,
Leicestershire. LE8 0RX
Tel: 0116 279 2299
Email: books@troubador.co.uk
Web: www.troubador.co.uk/matador
Twitter: @matadorbooks

ISBN 978 1789017 304

British Library Cataloguing in Publication Data.
A catalogue record for this book is available from the British Library.

Printed and bound in Great Britain by 4edge Limited
Typeset in 11pt ITC Giovanni by Troubador Publishing Ltd, Leicester, UK

Matador is an imprint of Troubador Publishing Ltd

Dedicated to the three wonderful Divas in my life: my mother Irene, wife Carol and daughter Kira

Our Souls
Are still the same forever, but adopt
In their migrations ever-varying forms…
We too ourselves, who of this world are part,
Not only flesh and blood, but Pilgrim souls…

Ovid: Metamorphoses

Foreword

A *Song for Demeter* was initially written as a college prose/poem dissertation circa 1976/7, with a general theme of life as a spiritual wasteland. It was forgotten about for forty years and then found and revised in 2016, with a 'Fool's journey' biography added to give the piece a more solid structure.

Consider the young Fool as he embarks on his life's journey, mindful of the suffering he observes in his daily life, especially when working in a home for elderly people. He is drawn to spiritual groups and listens to his friends' stories and experiences as they battle to make sense of their lives.

A *Song for Demeter* incorporates a mixture of youthful anecdotes, spiritual visions, poems, earthly conversations, allegorical stories and astonishing celestial revelations.

Richard Kemble
August 2018

ONE

Early Daze

HERE WE ARE then, a new day. Birds are pecking at my brain. I can feel them inside me. They will not stay for long: a few cells to chew, a little marrow to swallow and then they will be gone, until tomorrow. They like to prolong my torture.

My room is dark. The world is grey. Little pieces of death obsess me. Black socks for example. It is hardly surprising that I can determine no real spiritual direction when my feet meander darkly across the bright paths laid down for me to follow. I must wear red socks in future, or walk barefoot, so then I can run fleet-footed into crimson sunsets and find out where the true gods do lay.

A clock preaches quarter to nine. Outside the traffic snarls. I must be sure it does not get me.

In the late 1940s my mother Irene was a visionary in the sense that she was a vegetarian and followed a nature cure lifestyle that was considered most cranky. Her big mistake was to marry Geoffrey, who was far more interested in becoming a trance medium and channelling an 18th century monk than in caring for his wife. When the 'monk' tried to strangle her one day that signified the end of the marriage but by now I was on board, by all accounts a lively five-year-old.

When I was little I had a recurring dream, being a toddler trying to find my daddy. I would climb over fences and wander through gardens on the St Paul's Cray estate, feeling distraught trying to find him. In retrospect I never did 'find' my father who was always cool and detached from me although we did finally connect somewhat in his dotage.

Perhaps unsurprisingly Geoffrey also had a non-relationship with his own father Edward (Ted), who was highly critical of his wife and son for being such over-enthusiastic spiritualists. Ted considered them both as being, "Away with the fairies."

In the mid 1950s matrimony was considered a religious pact and divorce not only sinful but therefore very rare. When my mother told her parents she was divorcing Geoffrey they were shocked. The family would be shamed! My father would not comply with the notion of divorce, saying he would never divorce Irene. My mum was caught between a rock and a hard place: If she ran off with Fred, her first true love, she ran the risk of losing me. If she stayed with Geoff then life was so soulless she faced the prospect of putting her head back inside a gas oven. What should she do?

Mum went to an old gypsy clairvoyant/medium who plucked her off the end of a queue and told her in no uncertain terms to pursue love: so mum chose love.

However, when my mother finally left Geoffrey to live with Fred it was still a considerable surprise to everyone concerned to find Geoffrey fighting in the law courts to have full custody of me. Initially the court judgement went against my mother and I had to go to live with Geoffrey and my nana Bertha at Abbey Wood. This threatened separation became a significant primal moment in my life and I went into a deep shock. I cried for days as no child wants to be without its much-loved mother and then I became ill with pneumonia.

Eventually I did go to live with my paternal grandparents for a few months and Bertha was very kind to me but I was both resentful and vengeful. My eyes had been opened to the harsh realities of life and I don't think I was ever the same again.

On appeal the Law Courts reversed their judgement on condition that mum lived with her parents, so like a yo-yo I found myself back with my mother, now living at Eltham Park.

Bearing in mind the children's television shows that we watched in the fifties, like *Bill and Ben the Flowerpot Men*, it is a wonder we are not all verbally retarded, with the high-pitched incomprehensible language that we endured as tots.

"Awmaw."

"Hullowlittleweed."

"Hwcpcumminupwarway?"

Not that the Wooden Tops or Andy Pandy were any better but at least Pinky and Perky were pretty cool pigs.

My granddad Jack was very genial but had a spooky vibe. Like my father he was also a spiritualist and earnestly read his theosophy books. I remember him wagging his finger in the air and saying, "There might be another family living in our house but in a different space and time." I would nervously glance around the room and be comforted by familiar objects and wonder what on earth he was talking about.

Grandpa was my favourite playmate. Every night after he came home from work we would stare intently at the television and play our advert game, to see who would be the quickest to guess an advert. So, you would get a glimpse of a washing machine and roar 'Persil' or 'Daz' and keep a tally of who was winning, which was usually granddad. He hated to lose at anything and would sulk if I had the temerity to beat him at crib. Inadvertently playing crib taught me to count: fifteen – two, fifteen – four, fifteen – six, fifteen – eight, fifteen – ten and one for his knob!

Every week granddad would spend hours studying his pools coupon but I do not recall him ever winning anything. Sometimes he would let me fill in a line but I never brought him any luck. My favourite grandpa memory is heading off to the woods to pick blackberries. We would race to fill up some jam-jars and then fetch our berries home for nan to make her jam.

By the actions of his acrimonious divorce Geoffrey had completely alienated himself from my family. Non-communication with my mother did not seem to bother him too much. He focused on winning my affections by giving me a good time whenever we met up. Although emotionally detached he was kind to me and spoilt me with an array of fun activities. We went to Dreamland at Margate, travelled to football games and saw lots of great films like, *The Guns of Navarone* and John Wayne cowboy movies.

One day I had earache. It was excruciating. My father said, "Oh we will soon take care of that." He rubbed his hands quite vigorously and placed his right hand on my ear. His hand was like a furnace. I gasped that his hand could be so hot. After about a minute he changed hands and to my astonishment his left hand was like ice. My ear went completely numb and my earache vanished. So thus, I witnessed first-hand a minor miracle, performed by my outlawed father, the renowned spiritualist clairvoyant and healer. Rather oddly he never tried to teach me his supernatural skills.

My first school memory is of having a fight with a kid called Baxter. He had been bullying me, so one day I snapped and turned on him in the school playground. We wrestled around on the ground like two puppy dogs. Then I found myself on top so I repeatedly smashed his head against the ground until someone dragged me off him. The point being that I exulted in hurting him. I probably would have killed him if I could. He never attempted to bully me again. I hope I did not cause him any brain damage.

We moved to Forest Hill in 1961 after a terrible clash between my mother and grandmother Lily. I stood frozen in horror as my two maternal figures laid into each other in the small kitchen at Crookston Road. Kettles and pots were flying around as all the grievances that had been bubbling under the surface for countless years came tumbling to the surface. Eventually I recovered from the shock sufficiently to ease my raging mum out of the kitchen and up to her room. They did not talk to each other again for nearly twelve years.

On my last day at Deansfield Primary School I walked home with Pamela Rigby who said to me, "Bad riddance to good rubbish." I took it as a compliment. It is rare at such a young age to have someone sum you up in this manner. I thought it quite eloquent really. I think my teachers were secretly pleased to see the back of me.

Forest Hill was like a concrete jungle when compared to leafy Eltham. I missed running free in the woods, climbing the trees and having easy access to the vast Oxleas Meadows. Being in South London had its compensations: my pal Robin and I marvelled at the wonderful steam engines that rumbled through the train station like fiery dragons and we spent many happy hours together crossing off their serial numbers in our *I spy* train books.

My first crime was to break into my secondary school on a Sunday morning to retrieve some of my detention slips. If you received more than three detentions per week you would be caned by the housemaster and your parents were informed. The caning never bothered me too much; it hurt but I could bear it by wearing my football shorts under my trousers to alleviate my suffering. The embarrassing bit would be having to explain to my mum why I was getting so many detentions, so removing the detention forms was expedient. On a Sunday morning, I would call in on the school on my way to the park to play football. I would clamber through a window that I had left open and surreptitiously flit around the school and up the stairs to the staff room. Sometimes the caretaker would be on site so I had to be careful not to be seen. The staff room was fascinating but I did not linger. I would fish out my detentions from the box and then slip discreetly out of school.

Serving a detention was not unpleasant, usually an opportunity to do neglected homework. I liked the opportunity to write a story but the fascist teachers would often force you to write lines, which was a pure waste of time.

Being the only vegetarian kid at my comprehensive school was not at all cool. My so-called mates made rabbit faces and noises every day as I sat down with my salad and mash. So I ate wagon wheels at the tuck shop and got spotty instead.

It seems a little odd to me now that my grandmother Bertha, a devout spiritualist, should channel a Roman Catholic nun in her automatic writing; for on the mortal coil a devout catholic would be highly unlikely to participate in a seance. When I read the automatic writing, there was no doubting Sister Therise's enthusiasm and eagerness to describe her life beyond the veil; how the Master Jesus emanated such a wondrous love as he greeted heavenly newcomers, with an abundance of light glistening from him like the brightest of gems.

Sister Therise implored my downtrodden grandmother to bear her burden of sorrow with great joy, for it was such a blessing to do God's work, to ever alleviate the suffering of the bereaved, or tend to the weary who were finding the way heavy going.

Sister Therise described the sheer beauty of the spirit wild flowers, writing that each and every flower had a special meaning and that one day Bertha would understand and know for sure that God had a purpose for her that would enable her to go forward in freedom to do the work of her heart's desire. It was sweet to read that the good sister would gather some wild flowers on her walks and place them at Bertha's table, a gesture of love for she knew that her 'pupil' would love the flowers – even if she were unable to see them.

In my teens I would occasionally hop on two buses across to Abbey Wood, dutifully visiting my dad and grandmother but sans any wild flowers. If I close my eyes I can still see Bertha, my clairvoyant grandmother, answering the front door and turning to exclaim to my father, "I told you he would be coming today!" That always made me feel like running away. I wanted my visit to be my random choice, my free will, not an event already plotted on the board game of life. Why couldn't they be like normal people?

However, instead of rebelling I would sit down meekly to sup tea and biscuits and answer Bertha's questions about my progress at school. After listening to my negative tirade of school woes Bertha would tell me not to worry: "You will be fine my dear." If only I had her confidence. But now she is long gone, despite my father's prolonged healing, yet another victim to cancer:

I hurried to see you
as sand sifted through the funnel,
accumulating precious grains of time.
I wanted to point to you and say,
'So this is the web you have spun for yourself
in which you will wither and die.'
But I was four hours late to kiss your ghost goodbye.

And what am I doing here typing black letters upon a frozen page? Is it all a reflection of my inner disease?

In the big wide world the USA were at war with Vietnam. I would go on the protest marches in London and join in the chanting of, 'Ho, Ho, Ho Chi Minh.' Then on the following Monday, I would decorate the school corridors with the protest leaflets. They would stay up for a few hours and then my housemaster would call me into his office and demand that I take them all down.

I found school work hard going, my concentration being all over the place so after yet another uproarious classroom antic, I left school shortly before my 17th birthday. My housemaster said to me, "It's not working, is it?" I had to agree and promptly started a succession of city jobs that were totally unsuited to my distractible personality. I sucked at all of them: office junior; accounts clerk; Tippex salesman; container controller; and a clerical position at the Financial Times.

Good morning! The day is grey again. How can we brighten up our lives? It says in the paper you can win a brand new car; play the lottery. How about a face lift madam, or a tummy tuck, a nose job, or a boob reconstruction? Fix that bald patch sir, or have tablets for your premature ejaculation. You can be whatever you want to be and you can have it now. Just sign on the dotted line and trust in me.

Not being at school had considerable compensations. It was wonderful to have some money at the beginning of each month to spend as I cared. I travelled all around London, sometimes with friends but often alone, to see my favourite blues groups play in pubs and small venues: John Mayall's *Bluesbreakers* with Peter Green, Long John Baldry with a young Rod Stewart; Eric Clapton in *Cream*, *Ten Years After*, *Fleetwood Mac* and best of all, the amazing Jimi Hendrix at the Bromley Court Hotel.

I think it cost me fifteen shillings to see *The Jimi Hendrix Experience*. It was one of Jimi's early gigs in Britain and he blew us all away playing a mixture of blues standards and Dylan songs with his guitar behind his back, over his head and using his teeth to pluck the strings.[1]

She met him in the office, poor thing. There he stood, blank-eyed and distant. She liked him straight away but he was coated in reserve and appeared to hanker after his shadow as if it were the most natural place to be. On his first day he slunk behind the chief clerk as she introduced him to the team. Formally, he shook their hands. Before it was her turn she took off her glasses. A few minutes later he had taken her heart. She felt elated for she knew she had made a real contact but she had not seen the dark entity behind his half smile.

Slowly this fragmented young man began to grow in the office and she gradually found him catching her eye. His rather stern look would sometimes break into a smile as he became less tense with the passing of days. They spoke together sometimes at the Xerox machine, saying hello or mumbling work talk. It was always a bit of a strain.

Then one day they found themselves in the same compartment of a train. He said he was going to meet a friend. She knew it was a lie but just smiled. She wondered if he had another girlfriend. They talked freely, a sudden blurting of words. They both lived in south east London and no he was not going out with anyone and neither was she.

He was eighteen, already quite an accomplished failure. He had been slung out of school and was now into his third job. He hated it. He said he liked books and was football mad. She supported Arsenal like her dad. He offered to take her to a game and she said yes she would like to go. He had his own flat, this surprised her, and he collected obscure American records. He said his hair was short because he had to get it cut for the job.

She was a year younger than him and liked dancing in the clubs. He pulled a face. She had worked for the company for about nine months. It had been alright, a bit of a drag. As he talked she listened to the sound of his voice. She wanted to touch him but he was still very distant, this sad-eyed boy in a blue mohair suit.

A few days later they went on their first date. He seemed in another world this time. They watched a show called *Hair* and emerged arm in arm. He must have mustered some strength whilst in the shadows.

Over the next few weeks she waited for him patiently but he never quite drew near. Did he not like her? Slowly she reached out for him and at last he answered her call. Now she could touch him and feed him her love. The passion burned strong. She housed dreams where they would both settle down and live together in a loving way. She could sense a strength in him which only she could nurture. But then inexplicably he would turn on her and threaten to throw her out of his life. Up risen he rejected her and sought for whatever was real to him. He would return to the fold of his confident friends and with them play at being different personas and seek the mystery of other girls. Then broken and in misery he would return to her and claim her for his own, saying she was the only reality he had. Everything else would choke in his throat.

Bound by his weakness he gave her all the love he had. During this time she held him close to her comforting him with her presence. Then just as she began to feel secure about him once again he became restless and rejected her. It was as if he were scared of his future responsibilities.

Her tears laid her to waste. The same cycle turned over and over. The love they had felt became more veiled. Her barriers went up, she could take it no more. She hardened her heart to him but still she could not help but give. Hardness replaced the lamb of her love and he left her for good, shocked and numb.

Oh I'm just a butterfly
Living my life by my butterfly code
I fly from heart to heart
Giving my love to each open rose.
Will you love me if I settle on you,
Love me enough to let me go?
Or would you trap me in a jar,
Would you kill my butterfly soul?

◈

Playfully Jackie flaunts herself in front of a mirror.

"Oh! I wish I were thin. I mean really thin. I hate being fat like this."

"But you are not fat."

"Oh yes I am. Not as bad as I once was, before you met me. Ha! Now if you had seen me then!"

"But it hardly changes you, does it?"

"Of course it does. I really hate myself when I am fat."

"But you are not fat."

"I am."

"You're not. How can you be so stupid? You only weigh about eight stone."

"Well anyway, I'm going on a diet. Five hundred calories."

"What for? You are perfectly alright as you are. In fact you are quite thin."

"Well, I want to be ever so skinny... ever so."

"Why have you got such a phobia about it?"

"I haven't."

"I think you have."

"Oh you don't know what you are talking about."

"So you want to disappear then, do you? Or do you want to die a tragic death? In that case we should put you on a barge like Guinevere, skinny as a rake, drifting out to sea, returning to her maker."

"Oh shut up. You don't understand. I just feel better when I am skinnier, that's all."

"Why can't you just be normal. Not forcing anything, just being normal."

"It is natural for me to be skinny."

"Eh?"

"Wouldn't it be lovely not to eat at all!"

She said, "You never say you love me anymore!"
I answered, "Oh! but I do love you."
"No you don't!"
"Err… Yes I do."
"No you bloody well don't!"
And she stormed out of the door.

I didn't know what to say.
Was it that time of month,
when no matter what I did,
or didn't do,
I would be crucified
come what may?

Perhaps if I bought her some flowers,
or gave her some chocolates,
or took her to see a film,
one of those sloppy rom coms
that she seemed to like so much…
Maybe I could turn this around?
When she came back
I made a mistake.

I reached out a hand.
"Don't you touch me," she snarled.
"Don't think that you can crawl around me
as easily as that!"

Then she announced, "It's over!"
She put on her coat;
checked her face in the mirror;
twirled her bag over her shoulder
and flounced out of the room,
slamming the door after her, like thunder.

In the mid-sixties I met Steve in the covered end of our local football club. He was dressed in his mod gear, a loose-fitting parka, tight jeans and a sharp shirt. With his quick wit and Machiavellian manner it was like meeting a fellow spirit. Steve was always fun to be around, even if the jokes were too often at my expense.

Steve would invite me over to his Sidcup stomping ground and I met John and his other cronies. It was like stepping into the fast lane. I would later describe this initiation as being at the University of Tarrant and Hall. If you wanted to hang with Steve's crowd you had to work hard at fitting in. This meant wearing the right clothes, having an expensive haircut, spending lots of money and buying your mentors plenty of drinks!

We would travel across London to buy the cool American rhythm and blues records that would later be described as Northern Soul. There were the usual pub scenes, gigs, restaurants and all-night parties but really the scene was all about having Steve dominating centre stage, like a well-oiled theatre production. We all had our parts to play in the ongoing dramas, with me cast in a subordinate role as one of Steve's stooges, a bit like a well-dressed Baldrick.

One of Steve's crew was Colin, a genial, generous guy from a well-to-do family, who was always getting himself into scrapes. Colin would be forever stoned and duly crash his cars into ditches or do odd things like drive straight over roundabouts. We would spend the weekend at his parents' country home at Paddock Wood, playing snooker amongst ourselves, and try in vain to pull the local girls because they invariably objected to Steve's caustic wit. It took a lot to rankle Colin but Steve would bait him mercilessly until one night Colin laid him out with a vicious right hand.

I would occasionally set up some jolly japes such as faking an invitation from the AAA for Steve to run a mile at the Crystal Palace athletic arena. Receiving the invitation appealed to Steve's vanity because he always craved a sportsman's status, to be on a par with his buddy John, but Steve could barely walk a mile let alone run it. For weeks he would try to figure out if the invitation was real, or not. I would fan the vanity flames a bit but then lampoon him by saying things like, "You should be really honoured that you have been given this opportunity. Do you think you can actually get around the track without taking a breather?" Or, "Someone must have recommended you... or have they invited the wrong Steve Tarrant?"

In time, my own jaunts with Steve gradually faded as I took my studies more and more seriously. When I finally went to college I deliberately split from my much-loved Mephistopheles figure, never to see him again.

Sometimes the oppression is very heavy, blacking out all light from day. It weighs upon the mind, pulling down the vision so that one becomes preoccupied with trivial matters. Or you feel like a rat crawling from its hole, the stench of a filthy street being a kind of queer empathy. Everything threatens, dragging you down. A man offering a frivolous, 'Good morning' makes you feel like stabbing him in the back.

It was late spring, 1971 and the Pink Floyd were premiering Atom Heart Mother at the Crystal Palace bowl. I went with my school buddy John. The queues were enormous so John and I decided to forego the entrance fee and leapt over a gate. We quite easily outran the security guards and joined the throng on the hill.

I remember some of the acts. 'Mountain' were a bluesy American group, very professional. Rod Stewart and the Faces did their ramshackle act. Their guitars seemed to be out of tune but 'Maggie May' was fun and everyone seemed to join in. 'Elvis' turned up in a huge American car. He was quite convincing but opted not to sing. (I think it was really Shakin' Stevens.)

After the Faces performed John and I wandered off to stretch our legs. The backstage security was lax so we drifted through the gate and climbed up the steps of a portacabin. I was used to crashing journalist enclosures from my sojourn at The Isle of Wight festival. Indeed the portacabin turned out to be the press room with about twenty journalists crammed in interviewing Rod and the Faces. There was a table full of booze so John and I helped ourselves to a glass full of vodka and lime and watched Rod play with his hair as Ronnie Wood fronted the press. I recall the room being very smokey and the Faces were indeed very small!

After another big glass of vodka it was announced that the Floyd were finally about to perform so we joined the reporters as they queued up to watch at the side of the stage. An embarrassed guy told John and I that there was not enough room at the inside of the stage for all the press and the Floyd family members but would we mind watching from just outside by the speakers? We duly acquiesced and watched in wonder from our premier position as weird smoke poured out from the small lake in front of the stage. Then the group started to play but standing by the speakers was deafening so we had to plug our ears with paper to drown out the sound.

Without Syd Barrett the Pink Floyd were a bit boring to watch but beneath the lake something was stirring that looked like a monster of sorts. But then nature started to intervene and I was desperate for a pee. I had to crouch down at the back of the speaker and use my glass as a receptacle. I don't know what John did. I expect he just laughed at me. But then the heavens opened up and it poured with rain. Very irresponsibly I lifted a cover up from the speakers, so John and I remained dry while the paying punters were getting drenched. We were lucky the speakers did not blow!

My last memory of the event was listening to the encore of Syd's 'Astromine Domine', which sounded just wonderful when drunk and was much better than the worthy but unexciting 'Atom Heart Mother'. Sadly, all the fish in the lake died as a result of the noise and pollution.[2]

High up on Shoreham hill two young men drift around like castaways on another frequency. One gazed, as if through Samuel Palmer's eyes, at the yellow rapeseed billowing in the distance, with sheep grazing on those ancient hills like little puffs of smoke. In wonder he held a branch that had somehow morphed into his arm and glistened with its sub-atomic energy; a mini universe of magical colour. Later he watched absorbed, as a magnificent Buddha sat in the lotus position amongst the clouds in the sky.

Meanwhile Robin embraced a tree like a lover, giving a different meaning to flower power, whilst the breeze spoke to us in tongues.

In this aquarium the cars look like fish. Gliding by, grunting, hungrily eying the pedestrians. Occasionally they would rise to the surface and swallow a body or two and then spit out the bones upon the sidewalk. Growling they consume the air and exhume poisonous oxides. Their tiny slaves polish them lovingly. They are almost real. But the big fish eat the little fish and the celestial fish is torn to shreds leaving only a few tattered bones for the world to adore.

It said in the paper that he went on the rampage following her spoor down the high street. Earlier he had selected his victim and followed her amid the crowd. His black hair, cut short like a modern-day Mohican, set him apart from the crowd. Faces turned to look at him but he did not see them, he was too intent on her. She sensed the danger in a supermarket.

The hair on her neck prickled as she passed through the check-out but once outside she cast aside her groceries and made a dash for her car. He followed swiftly but she slammed the door shut just in time and locked him outside. He glared at her through the front windscreen window and then withdrew into the crowd. On this occasion the wolf was thwarted but the poor deer was left fraught with fear.

TWO

Why are we Sleeping? A Time of Despair

IN MY LATE teens, ever influenced by my rock-star idols, I read how Robert Fripp of *King Crimson* was a devotee of the Russian/Armenian sage Gurdjieff and followed up this interest by reading a primer about this extraordinary man who had wowed many western intellectuals circa 1920–1940s. This book shook me out of my general malaise for I identified with his broad concept that we were sleep-walking our way through life, perhaps only awakening on rare occasions such as being in love, or on being bereft of a loved one.

Gurdjieff would give his band of followers exercises to keep them alert and 'awake'. They had to avoid any routines and had to watch themselves as if from outside their body. So I would practise watching myself doing my daily actions, such as walking to Forest Hill railway station; up the hill, past the church and council flats, and would sometimes take a different route to avoid the 'sleep walk' as I called it. Of course if Mike, my flat mate, was with me there would be no self-analysis as we would be too busy ogling the young ladies on the station platform.

I would deliberately get out of bed on the wrong side, eat with my left hand and sometimes even walk backwards! At work I would watch myself go through my work routines, such as phoning Liverpool docks to check on a container ship's arrival and tick off on my computer handout my given quota of container codes. The trouble with playing this analytical game was allowing myself to become a split persona as I was increasingly separate from my work self. I had no idea who this puppet was, or who pulled his strings. As I watched myself meander my way through life my doubts grew and grew. It seemed to me that the most successful guys were fully integrated into their work mode, whereas I was fractured and functioned poorly when compared to them. I just knew that I would never be able to cut it as a computer clerk as it was too meaningless to me, so I quit the job before I was sacked.

Gurdjieff implied that most of us journey through life as if we were asleep on a train going nowhere.[3]

When we are born we are put upon a train and without knowing are taken for a very long ride. Few people ever made the effort to leave the train despite the fact that no-

one knew where the train was bound. People developed what can only be described as train mania, gauging their progress by the train's momentum as it rolled along the line. No-one could see the train as a whole, for they had all become an integral part of its overall structure.

People began life as lively little passengers, gradually learning the train's quirks and mannerisms. Then they decided how best they could help to maintain the train and maybe aspire to eventually own their own compartment. They then spent most of their lives working as a cleaner, porter, guard, refreshment man, inspector or even as a driver. After this toil they earned the right to be a passenger for the rest of their days until they reached their final destination. Then they left the train at a certain station and no-one ever saw them again. These mysterious stations were feared by the passengers. Some even liked to pretend that they did not exist. Others lived in total fear that the next stop might be their personal terminus.

No-one, least of all the driver knew what lay ahead on the line. The train always rushed full tilt into the darkness. However, on occasions the train's journey would be delayed by all kinds of irksome troubles. For example, the coal might be a poor lot, or the food would run low, or the oil might clog. Whenever these troublesome incidents occurred the train would be in uproar. The third-class passengers would blame the first-class and the first-class passengers would blame the third and the second-class passengers would be blamed from both directions. Then a new engine driver would be elected to take control of the train after promising all the various factions that he would be able to solve everyone's grievances.

The engine drivers themselves were a peculiar brand of people, usually selected from the first-class compartments and thus with very little knowledge of second-class, let alone third-class passengers. They would always have a grandiose, knowledgeable air about them and would often state that they knew exactly where the train was bound, claiming that they were on a familiar loop or such nonsense. Strangely, the passengers always seemed to believe them as if they had to rely on someone's assertions. The engine driver would frequently baffle the train people with a series of complex time schedules based on the train's revolutions per thousand miles, energy consumption and so on. These schedules were for ever being modified or revised as the train suffered unseen difficulties. On these occasions the engine driver would always assume an air of absolute confidence.

Among the passengers there would be much dissension regarding how the train should be run. The first-class passengers were generally all for their own comfort with strong interest in the train's prestige. The second-class passengers frequently had a laissez-faire attitude; they did not care what happened so long as they did not have to sit in the third-class compartments. The third-class passengers bitterly resented the first-class passengers and demanded an end to all class distinctions, proposing the same seats for everybody. However, their image was often spoilt by a rowdy faction whose only interest focused on the train's speed. Perhaps the most frightening section were those *people who believed in their train's right to knock smaller trains off their track so that they could then run on their lines. Thankfully such opportunities were few and far between.*

On rare occasions the train might get derailed but usually they chugged along, patched up and in dire need of a good overhaul, with the passengers totally unaware of the train's real difficulties. Asleep, the passengers allowed themselves to be taken nowhere by leaders who, overwhelmed by their own sense of importance, actually believed they knew the train's destiny.

So, instead of being a means of travel, the train became the sole reason for living. He who came to redirect the train was himself derailed. The train that ran over his body paused, drank his blood, ate his flesh and then rushed on into the darkness, somehow convinced that only this train, on this track, would lead its passengers into the light.

In retrospect reading about Gurdjieff was an important key that helped me inwards on my long search for self-discovery, although I could never comprehend his book, *Beelzebub's Tales to His Grandson.*

After a failed attempt to emigrate to Australia on the ten pound scheme, I decided to do something drastic. I craved excitement and wanted to explore the world, so after I had quit my office job I said goodbye to my friends and set off to Spain with a tent and a rucksack on my back.

I hitched rides in lorries and cars, racing my football pal Phil as we passed on through France and across the Alps. We had quickly realised it would be much easier to travel alone and indeed it was, until at last I reached our destination at Lloret de Mar and set up my tent at our designated campsite. I loved the warm Mediterranean Sea and spent my first day swimming and sunbathing, which was a big mistake for I suffered horrendous sun stroke and spent the next two days in a flu-like fever.

As planned we later met up with our friends who had booked a fortnights package holiday and the frolics began but I fell ill again and had to be cared for by the sisters of Santa Maria. I was obviously not used to the excessive bohemian lifestyle. I had planned to earn money in Spain by handing out leaflets for clubs, or perhaps serving in a bar but these ideas were never activated; they were always, *mañana*.

When one set of friends returned home, I set off to meet up with Steve and John in Calella but disaster soon struck for all my belongings, including passport and money, were stolen from me. I obtained a new passport at the British embassy in Barcelona and my parents sent me survival money but with my spirit somewhat broken I had to return to England and start all over again.

Back in London everything is conformity grey. In the city policemen walk watchfully by contemplating crime in pairs. Their uniforms are swallowed up by the dark night. Black cabs shuffle around sleazy corners picking up tarts like lots. Refuse bags, ominously silent, linger in shop doorways. A decaying body gulps down its meths. He does not see anymore. He is spiritually blind. He feels the burning in his throat grip him like a vice. He is fixed in this neon world.

The mournful moon glistens down on the red lights as guilty men resurface from the cinemas. Erections fading fast they hurry to catch the last train home, hoping to penetrate the dreams of their long-suffering wives.

Perhaps tomorrow they will have recovered their libido sufficiently to bound breezily into their city office to once again leer at the female staff. After all, they are the kings in this male dominated realm.

In the twilight world of the damned
curled lips glower in the darkness.
A limp hand deftly slices sordid shapes in the air,
beckoning bodies from their starched striped suits
to enter her cynical contemptuous lair.

At last a shape converges upon her
and disappears through her dark door.

Later this bedraggled figure is seen retching in the gutter.
What kind of gesture is this to the world?

How hard it is to live with a distorted image. When I do wicked or cruel things you reflect these ugly actions right back at me. I can't stand it! I can't live with this image no matter how true it is of me. How do I change? How does one begin to improve, to purify?

I can see that it is far easier to go down a notch or two and simply accept being the shit that you are, rather than attempt to ascend in consciousness. Then I could hold up my hands and say, "Yep, that's me. I'm sorry but that is who I really am."

Then you get on with this diminished notion of yourself, and learn to live with this persona, warts and all.

So here he is, my alter ego. His room smells of damp. The gutters need repairing. Unfinished paintings litter his room. Another failure is already furnished in his head. A library gathers dust. He does not want to read, he wants to be heard but he has nothing to say. The fury builds inside of him. Frustration gathers like an angry storm. Who shall he kill today? His mother? No, she has been dead ever since she festooned him upon the world. He has assaulted his girlfriend five times already. She enjoys it. His inner violence is what attracts her to him.

Here she comes now, sweet lamb. She has his dinner in her hand. Her typist fingers open the door, she clickety clicks across the floor. In anger he goes at her with a knife. He writes tomorrow's headlines.

The blanket is over me again. I am safe and warm. No-one can hurt me here. I want to go to sleep. I want to return to the time before I awoke too soon from my deep infant slumber. The light is faltering now. I have been watching it dance around my room for the past half hour like a tiny shimmering spirit. Maybe If I lie very still it will enter my being and transform my dark thoughts into sparkling prisms of wonder. But with each passing moment the light moves further away until I am finally left alone to lament my time without grace.

After Spain I am now living with a butcher's family in Catford. They tolerate my vegetarian diet without fuss. I have been offered work in my friend's furniture shop.[4] It was a big store selling old and new furniture, a kind of work bastion for wretched souls like me, or for students who had dropped out of university and were biding their time. I would stand in the furniture shop staring blankly outside at the bleak walls of

Forest Hill Station, waiting patiently for a customer to serve. Then suddenly I would lurch into action, polishing or dusting furniture whenever the owner's wife slipped, ghost-like into the room, for she hated to see anyone idling their time away.

I think Bill, the owner, employed me on the grounds that I was a capable chess player who had nice manners but selling furniture was obviously not my forte. I was a lost soul. Beyond lost. I was the epitome of the walking dead.

One afternoon my angel came to rescue me. She came in the guise of an elderly lady wandering around the shop perusing low quality wardrobes at the back of the store. Keen to practise my salesman's spiel I directed her attention to a fake mahogany that had been recently polished. She did not appear too impressed but for some reason proceeded to tell me about her working day. She was a teacher of handicapped children. Her eyes lit up as she described how she had switched from being a primary school teacher to working with these special needs children. Absorbed, I just listened, admiring her passion.

Then she looked me straight in the eye and said, "You are wasted here. You should be doing what I do." Then with a smile she left the shop leaving me stunned for I knew she was absolutely right. A light had been switched on and I felt at long last that I had a real goal to aim for.

But after a few days this glistening hope soon began to fade as a ghastly realism set upon me. I had been a total failure at school and I had struggled to succeed at any of my work opportunities so how could I expect to become a teacher? Plus, being an only child I had never had any contact with children. They were quite alien to me. It seemed an impossible ambition and I shuddered at the thought of going to college to re-take examinations.

Despite an avalanche of negative thoughts I somehow kept this kernel of hope alive at the back of my mind and I began to explore the possibilities of taking O-levels at evening classes.

In the summer wanderlust hit me again and I went with my girlfriend Jackie and pal Pat to experience life on a kibbutz in Israel. Beforehand I had a row with my GP who was furious with me for refusing a tetanus injection. He thought I was being negligent but I was acting on principle. I had thought long and hard about vivisection and regarded it as an evil doctrine. Why should innocent creatures be sacrificed for my life?

Israel was similar to Spain but hotter. I really enjoyed the farm-like kibbutz life, mainly picking fruit with the odd shitty job such as cleaning the empty swimming pool. We volunteers worked hard during the mild early morning and coped as best we could in the blistering mid-day heat. Then after lunch we had the rest of the day to ourselves. I was miserable though, for Jackie and I were not getting on. She was sure of herself and resisted my new-found spiritual concepts, probably thought I was being pseudo, so we spoke less and less. After we split I felt at a loss and did not know what to do with myself.

A snake creeps up upon a small bird.
She hears a rustle of movement and spreads her wings to escape.
Too late, for he has her in his jaws.
He crushes her freedom.

Soon she is scrubbing the floors,
cooks his meals,
irons his laundry
and turns out the lights for him.

She ponders her freedom.
Every day she feeds him a little poison
by opening her legs with a smile.
He catches a progressive dose and dies.

In the morning there is no washing up to do.
She looks around and sees her chains lying on the floor.
She is free!
She can do anything she wants to do!

She takes a huge leap into the air,
sails over the balcony and falls crushed to the ground.

I am told there is only today. Nothing else matters but this moment, and this, and this… I the mechanical being watch as the seconds tick on by. The clock now says ten thirty. What does that mean? That the sun has reached point x in the sky? The magnetism of gravity pulls us in ripples around the sun but are our emotions governed by the stars? Today I am influenced by Uranus, the erratic planetary system but what does all this astrology really mean? Perhaps deep within me lies every star, lying latent with expectation, waiting for my inner quest to begin.

Back in Blighty I enrolled at Lewisham College to resit my O- and A-levels. It took me two years to attain the appropriate grades. Unlike the other students, initially I helped myself to an illicit state grant. Every Tuesday I would dash out of the college at break time, hurtle down the high street, queue up, sign on the dole and then dash back to the college, sometimes arriving late for my next lesson, for occasionally I would be interviewed for a prospective job. If it was a rep's job, or sales, I would stammer and say how I would love to take the job but became very nervous when speaking to people and that handling money was a problem for me. Fortunately I was not interviewed very often. After two terms of playing this cat and mouse game I decided to quit taking the dole before getting into serious trouble with the authorities.

At first it was a real battle for me to learn how to concentrate on my studies for any extent of time. I had a quiet room to study in but my whole being itched to be off down the street to have some fun, to be free larking about with my friends. Frequently I would have to re-read my literacy texts, or my maths books several times to fully assimilate the words/ numbers as I battled what appeared to be a form of undiagnosed attention deficit syndrome. I suppose I was a bit like a junkie learning to live without a fix but in time my focus did gradually improve and I began to enjoy my studies.

I still cringe when I recall another part-time student job working as a porter in the local hospital. The head porter, a savvy old guy, seemed to delight in allocating me the most dreaded tasks. Fair enough that I had to empty the waste bins with the other porters but they never seemed to complain about the smell. For me it was a shock to my senses. It was as if their sense of smell had adjusted to the hospital stench. With my sensibilities intact, I was obviously not cut out to be a dustman.

Every week or so I would be despatched to the kitchen to support the kitchen staff. Preparing the food for hundreds of patients and staff would have appealed to me but the cranky Hungarian chef, with a crooked moustache, would always direct me to the stinking soup urn and order me to clean it out. Over a period of time various bones would be cast into the large urn for stock, supposedly for the soup to taste better. This stock would bubble away for days on end. It was my job to remove all the carcass and then to scrub out the urn as best I could. I would get covered in greasy fat and the stench was just awful. To make matters worse the nurses would point and smile at my misfortune from the opening to the canteen. I was not at all happy to be on public display.

Every morning after the early duties were completed the porters would all settle down in their staff room and sip their tea. They would smoke and gawk at the page three girls in newspapers like the *Sun*. I would discreetly get out one of my text books and read a page or two but then would invariably be turfed out to run an errand. Apparently it was okay to read the *Sun* but not Thomas Hardy. The head porter either did not like literature or did not like me.

By far the worst job was removing the dead bodies from the post mortem slab and sliding them into the freezer. Bear in mind this was a TB hospital: the stench was unbelievable. I would be retching before I had even seen the body. My survival technique was to take a huge breath of fresh air, dash into the room with my eyes half closed, help cover the body with the thick polythene cover and then dash out of the door again. There would be blood all over the place. My partner would think my little performance absolutely hilarious and would later entertain the other porters at my expense. None of the other porters bothered about the smell at all and were far more interested in the shape of any female naked body. I would then come rushing back into the room and we would lift the stretcher into the freezer room next door and hopefully heave the body into the fridge in one go before I needed to take another breath. Finally we would have to wash down the slabs to ensure they were clean for the next operation. With the body out of the way I could now breathe a little easier.

We were drilled that anything that had blood on it had to be taken to the incinerator. The smoke would billow from the tall chimney. I would wonder at the TB molecules being cast to the wind and hope that I was immune to this horrible disease.

In the summer of 1973 I found myself on the magical Isle of Iona, living on a croft. I lived in a tiny hut that I christened, 'The Wendy House'. It was not a very practical abode but I had a bed, it was warm enough and better than camping in the rain. More importantly it was cheap to rent. Every other week I travelled across Mull to Oban to sign on the dole and try to convince the guys at the job centre that I was incapable of work. They never did offer any employment to me, this strange guy up from London; I surmise I am better at acting daft than selling furniture.

Every morning I would go into John Black's house to wash and later I would feed myself in the barn using a little primus stove to warm up my very basic vegetarian food. I would amuse John by cutting up wild nettles from around his croft and digging out some thyme, thus making almost free soup, adding a dollop of Marmite for flavour.

John, the owner of the croft, would shake his head and say, "You need to eat some meat, mate."

Dilly, a hippy from Aberdeen, would play his flute and lure me on one of his jaunts climbing around the edge of the Iona rocks. It was fun playing this dangerous game. I remember shaking in fear as I wobbled over a chasm, my legs splayed out, unable to move with the sea breaking angrily below me. Somehow I rocked to and fro before lunging onto a ledge. It was my first dice with death. Dilly just laughed at me and shook his head at my inept climbing skills.

Much later, Stephen told me about a friend of his, I'll call him Max, who was born with a full memory of his previous lives. Apparently Max had refused to drink the cup of Lethes before his return to our mortal coil; this being a drink which causes all of us to forget our previous sufferings and to start our new life afresh. Max was thus very psychic, with open vision, being able to read people's past lives as well as his own.

Stephen had felt a real infinity with the holy Isle of Iona and asked Max if he had lived there in a previous life but Max informed him that he had a strong Irish connection from rural Ireland and it was the tranquil beauty of nature that Stephen longed for, which of course had a similar vibration to the peacefulness of Iona.

Hearing this story made me wonder if it was a gift or a curse to be reborn with such knowledge of previous lives? If you know that someone has made a calamitous decision that will seriously affect not only their own life but that of many others are you meant to interfere? Is that why you have been given this 'gift' of seeing? Or are you meant to pass through life without meddling, knowing that people have free will to make their own decisions and have to suffer the consequences of their foolish actions?

THREE

Introducing the Elderly and the Mystic

MY NEXT STUDENT job was working as a care attendant in an old people's home. I was not at all sure if I would be able to cope but I soon found that I had compassion for the elderly and enjoyed the staff banter.

On my first day working in the care home I had to help Danny bath 'Pop' who was allegedly the oldest man in England at the time, being 107, although the old scoundrel had no birth certificate to prove his age. Pop liked to suck on his clay pipe and tell stories about his midshipman days in the navy; how they would fire musket guns during sea battles. He was very astute for a man of his antiquity and loved to banter with Danny who would scold him for making an ashen mess with his pipe.

Being a Liberal Pop would always be in the paper during elections, with a smiling prospective candidate clinging onto his hand. Pop would bluster the virtues of Gladstone, or Lloyd-George, much to the delight of the local reporter.

I remember the clear skin of his broad back as he sat in the bath, with him telling me to hurry up applying the soap suds because he did not want to be late for his lunch. Hauling him out of the bath was not easy because he was a such dead weight.

Within weeks of Danny leaving the care home in a fit of pique, Pop died. I think he missed his care attendant sparring partner and had no reason to carry on anymore.

My mother and step dad Fred moved to Plymouth, pursuing their dream of living in the west country but it all went awry after mum had a kundalini experience which completely unhinged her. She had been doing some yoga breathing exercises on the floor and after a particularly deep breath through her nose her body went 'whoosh!' and she was never quite the same again! For nearly a year she became exceedingly psychic. Public transport was impossible because she could 'read' the minds of everyone she looked at and experience their unhappy emotions. She had to quit her public relations job because she was unable to type or take telephone messages, plus she unearthed a corruption conspiracy that eventually led to the whole department being closed down.

At night she would watch UFOs in the sky but she also suffered some awful astral attacks:

"Go away," she said. "You are not real."
The astral forces tried to seduce her.
They wanted her to become their servant;
she would earn a lot of money;
she would become famous.
"Go away," she said. "You are not real."

Then they bombarded her with a variety of threats.
She was terrified of snakes,
so venomous snakes hissed and slithered up her bed;
they were going to strike her head.
Despite her terror she dismissed them;
"Go away," she screamed. "You are not real."

They threatened to take away her sight.
They said she would go blind.
"Oh go away," she said. "You are not real."
But she took a peep at a banshee wailing at the window;
The blue grey torment shrieked at her;
a cackle of hatred.

She battled against evil on that long night
but she lost her sight in her right seeing eye.

Mrs Dowding, a diabetic, hisses in the shadows. She twitches in her permanent bossa nova, cursing the world, longing for the taste of sugar.

"I don't live here. I don't belong 'ere, do I? Course not. You know I don't. It's all that Annie Burnett's fault. She knocked me over this morning, she did, swore at me too. Called me a fucking old cow, she did. And that Sister Keenhan hates me, she does. I hate her 'n' all and I hate you." She rocks herself into a prolonged rage.

She sits in her room. Her husband is dead. He died yesterday morning at ten o'clock. They were inseparable. How she loved to hate him but now the bugger had gone. Who could she flay into now? He had mirrored her misery and she would scratch at the reflection with venom. Without him now she felt so empty. She was skating across the surface of the world with nothing to stop or hold her from falling over the edge.

She put on her stockings. It was such an effort. Once it had been so exciting to remove them one by one in front of him. Now the door was shut. No-one would enter. She was alone. Why was it so quiet? Where was his whining, ever complaining voice now? How she missed her throb of temper as she turned on him with vengeance!

The radio lay two yards away on the dressing room table but to her horror, it seemed too far. Panic stricken she rose to her feet and moved insect-like across the space. She pressed the button and the air came alive rescuing her from her own dark malady. For a few dreadful moments she had thought that she might also be about to die. She listened to the sounds, relieved, with a smile. She had found a little pocket of time.

The sun shone down on the red brick building. In the garden an old man sat on a bench staring far away into the distance. Nearby, two ladies exchanged pleasantries during their cigarette break.

"Was he drunk when he came in last night?"

"I dunno. Never 'eard 'im enter. I would 'ave been bloody annoyed if I 'ad."

"But don't you worry about him going out with the lads?"

"No. I couldn't care less what 'e did anymore."

"But you know what they are like when they all get together."

"Yeah. It makes me sick. They think they are so clever try'n' to get a bit on the side. I think 'e's pathetic. 'E don't even succeed in that! I wish 'e would, then 'e could clear out and I would 'ave 'im off my back."

"Oh but I hate it when my Joe comes in late. I don't tell him though. I pretend I don't care. I just go all hard on him. I never let him 'ave me either. That makes him go all narky. The worst bit about it is that I get all jealous when he's out. I wonder where he is and what he is doing. Always at the back of my mind I'm wondering whether or not he's got himself a bint. Sometimes 'e don't want to go, I can tell but it's like a ritual… Friday night out with the boys. And there's me stuck indoors doing the bloody ironing."

"I've tried all the obvious things, like going out all dressed up but he just laughs and says, 'Ave a good time luv!' Sometimes I wish he would knock me about a bit, at least that would show that he cared but he just sits there watching the bloody telly. I've been back to me mother's twice but it ain't fair on the kids. I think that got through to him a bit though. I even went to the yoga class last week, tying myself up in bleedin' knots trying to get a bit of weight off and he didn't even notice that I had left the house! Oh it's so hard but I still love him, I really do."

After my mother's extraordinary kundalini experience she and my step dad Fred returned to London. Quite quickly mum became a member of the Order of the Cross, an established mystery school of esoteric 'Christian' teachings, located in Kensington. [5] I accompanied my mother on her Sunday visits wondering what had she got herself into now? It was like attending a high Anglican church, filled with smiling but ageing vegetarians, sweetly uttering praises like, "Bless you my dear," as I struggled to explain who I was and why I was there. Everyone was exceedingly nice. I felt like a wretch.

I quickly gathered that all these people believed that Jesus was a holy Nazarene and thus a vegetarian who had experienced a normal birth. These revelations were from the founder, the Reverend John Todd Ferrier, who had passed away in 1943. My mother was very disappointed to have missed the opportunity to meet him. After about three visits my enthusiasm began to wane because the services were very formal and focused on little bits of the message like how Lazarus was raised from the dead but not really because it was an allegorical story.

In the kitchen mighty Flo slobbers over her pots and pans. She paws the food with her huge fleshy hands. The elderly residents, eating mechanically, often ask for more.

But Flo is not having a good day. At break time she lurches into the staff room.

"Nobody ever leaves nuffin' to us!"

"Nah!"

"Nothin'."

"Who looks after them? And who gets all the bleedin' money?"

"The relations get it."

"Yeah! I ask yer… The bloody relations!"

"Yes."

"I wouldn't mind but yah never see 'em until they drop dead and then they come swarming all over the bloody shop after the bleedin' money!"

"I should have thought ol' Flinders would have left us something."

"Who?"

"Mrs Flinders. You know the one with hydro… what's-it… the one with a big head."

"What the one with water on the brain, like?"

"That's the one."

"I didn't know she was dead. Iris never said anything and she always seems to know when they are about to pop off. She says they have a funny smell."

"Spooky it is."

"Anyways, I would have thought she would have left somefink to the staff for being so kind to her."

"She didn't 'arf take some looking after, 'n'all!"

"Those poor night staff!"

"Water on the brain, water in the bed, water everywhere!"

"Haa..nnah."

"We don't get nuffin'."

"One geezer comes once a week and stays long enough to get the Matron to sign off some money to him and then he's off! He doesn't even bother to see the old dear! Bloody cheek it is. They would slit your throat from ear to ear."

"Only one person ever left us something and that was Mr Dodd. He left us fifty quid. We gave it back to Matron 'cos when we doled it out we only had about thirty bob each so Matron bought the babies a telly, so they had somefink to look at."

"That's right."

"'Ere. Who was that fella in your kitchen earlier on, with that girl?"

"That was 'im. The bloody archy-tec. I can't stand the bloke and he knows it 'n'all."

"She can't say architect!"

"What did 'e want then?"

"I don't know. I don't speak to 'im anymore. I ignore 'im."

"Why's that?"

"Why's that! Bloody 'ell! 'e came into my kitchen and said, 'Where's the cook?' I said, 'There's more than one cook you know.' 'E looked down his nose at me and said, 'I don't want to speak to the assistant cook.' Assistant cook! I ask yer! I'm old enough to be 'is mother, the cheeky little swine."

"Yeah."

"Oh, John get your hands off of me! Sex mad you are. Only know about one 'fing!"

"Bloody bite him Flo!"

"Ahhh!"

"That'll teach him."

"Haa..nnah."

One eventful Sunday we met Antony Bates, who had been suspended from the Order of the Cross for being over challenging to the trustees. He was the bad boy of the Order and my mother hit it off with him straight away. We were invited to one of Antony's meetings at his big house in Kew Gardens.

Antony Bates was a mystical artist, very much in the style of William Blake.[6] He was also a fine communicator and I soon became quite engrossed in his esoteric 'Christian' teachings, which were all based on Todd Ferrier's revelations.

Antony's group met about once a fortnight at his house in Kew. I was somewhat cynical at first and looked for the flaws but then began to be absorbed by the mystic teaching. In all these esoteric matters you either resonate with what is being taught, or you don't.

Entering the artist's house was quite an experience because as soon as you crossed the threshold your senses became jangled by the array of colour, mystique and grandeur of the paintings on display all over the house. As you approached the stairs a statuesque Mercury, with wings on his heels, beckoned one heavenwards. A succession of family portraits, or of friends long passed over, lined the walls.

Mystical paintings depicting an esoteric interpretation of Christianity were prominent with a picture of Peter escaping from prison but indicating that he had to escape from a tomb in the shape of a cross. A forlorn willow tree symbolically depicted the agony of Gethsemane. Then a beautiful depiction of the state of angelic love, 'The City of Fragrant Roses', the red roses here being a symbol of love in a heightened walled city.

Walking into the splendidly ramshackle studio one's senses were again blitzed by the array of ideas presented in the paintings adorning the walls. A huge picture depicted the world in bondage to the illuminati, or the house of Ephraim, which dominated the room; with black people in chains, with a smiling Pope, monarchists and scientists dangling people on strings like puppets. But what really caught the eye were the downtrodden animals, for the animal kingdom was being exploited by everyone. The lowly creatures were sacrificed by the human race to appease their senses and appetites – the epitome of evil in our fallen wasteland of a world.

Penny explains the latest mishap in the dementia unit.

"Matron sent us this Korean girl who was doing her school work experience. Must have thought the kid needed some real experience handling shit and whatnot to see if she were up for the job.

"Anyhow, she was put on the late shift helping us put the 'babies' into bed. Luckily we only had a few accidents to deal with, so for once we had some time on our hands before leaving at eight o'clock.

"I said to her, go around the rooms and make sure their teeth are cleaned. Y'know, I showed her how we put their teeth in a glass with some Steradent. Then I left her to it.

Next morning I get a call from Sister in a right strop telling me to get over here quick, like. When I get in everyone's in a panic 'cos Tu-Shadi has only emptied out all the babies' dentures into a bucket and poured Steradent into the bucket to save time! So no-one knows whose teeth fit who!

"Well I know some of the dentures, like the Major's 'cos he's still got a few teeth at the back but tryin' to work out who the teeth belonged to was a nightmare. I'm going, "Try these Daphne," and the old girl sort of chugs the teeth around her mouth but they obviously didn't fit. It was like trying to fit a shoe for bleedin' Cinderella!

"Old Flo, bless her, made a load of porridge at breakfast so at least the old dears could eat something. The funny thing is without their teeth you couldn't make out what they were saying! The only one who was alright was Joyce because she had her initials on the back of her dentures. What a palaver eh!"

An old lady walks down the polished corridor. Disinfectant stifles the air. She waves her stick. "Ooh! Ooh, the birds, the birds. Get these birds away from me!"

Rose has just come on duty. "What birds me darlin'?"

"These pigeons. They keep flying at me?"

"Oh really! Well you be sure they don't shit on you then, won't you!"

I met Mark at the Order of the Cross and we became close friends. He was the son of a Baronet who had been taught at a boarding school military academy. I think the general family plan was for Mark to eventually attend Sandhurst to train as an army officer. However, Mark had alternative ideas for he dropped out of school and opted out of anything traditional.

He was always very extroverted, an avowed naturist he enjoyed performing his yoga/Tai chi exercises completely naked at Green Fairs, preferably smeared with green paint. When he visited us I would plead with Mark to keep his underpants on whilst exercising in the communal gardens but at Pen Ponds, in Richmond Park, he would ignore me and strip off to go for a swim despite the 'No Swimming' notices.

In terms of confidence Mark was quite the opposite of me, for he always had full assurance in everything he did, a typical Aries in that regard. For example, he would read a few chapters of a book on homeopathy and immediately become an authority on the subject. He could not restrain himself from lecturing Carol, which would irritate Carol no end for she had spent years studying homeopathy and later taught at a homeopathic college.

Mark always seemed compelled to push the physical boundaries so it was no real surprise that he became a keen mountaineer. We were all devastated when one winter he fell to his death on Ben Nevis, leaving behind a baby son and an older boy from his previous relationship. I wept like a girl at his funeral whilst his rather noble family kept their feelings firmly under control with a stiff upper lip.

Ena has been to the gynaecological clinic for her annual check-up.

"My gawd it was awful. I was so nervous. I sat in the waiting room and this posh looking lady comes in and sits next to me. I goes, 'I dread coming here.'

She says, all calm like, 'Oh you get used to it. I have to come here on a regular basis because I have a prolapsed bladder.'

I looked at her bemused. She said she had botox injected into her bladder to tighten it up a bit!

'Oh,' I said. Didn't know what to say really.

Then by way of explanation she said, 'It's not my main problem. I've got a loose bowel.'

'Oh,' I goes, 'do they inject it with botox?'

'Don't be stupid,' she replied, 'they fitted my bowel with a pacemaker!'"

There is a stir in the community room where blind Harry sits in his chair muttering a dirge unto himself.

"Oh I'm ill. Oh I'm ill. Won't someone help me?

I feel bad. I feel bad. Can't someone help me?

Oh I'm bad. Oh I'm bad. Won't someone help me?"

His eyes are lost mists, fogging the pale gaze. Forgotten he sits in discomfort until at last the dam breaks and a little yellow brook gushes across the floor.

The women are shocked. They shake their heads, mortified.

"Never known anything like it, I ain't. Disgusting he is." A few look on in dull sympathy.

After a while Harry is frogmarched away in disgrace. The stream is mopped up and silence prevails again for a while.

On the day of the 'Followers of The Way' meetings group members gathered together on the first floor studio of Antony's house. Chairs were scattered around but I usually preferred to sit on the floor with my back to the wall. The characters would enter the studio one by one; there was Peter, an eccentric Old Harrovian, who tuned pianos for a living. He would soon fly to St Petersburg to renovate the cathedral organ. His partner Doris was not a mystic at all but a rabid animal rights campaigner who would rage at animal suffering at some point during the meeting. They had a vegetarian dog that would defy its owners' dietary designation by hurdling over the garden gate, making its way down the road to the local store and stealing a bone from the butcher's shop.

Francis would turn up with one or two of her children and set out some vegan food. Avril, who would later run the group for a while, would usually be in discussion with my parents and I would often chat with a music hall entertainer who played harmonica like an English Larry Adler.

Antony's wife Sita might bless us with her presence wearing one of her beautiful saris. Mike would usually be in attendance, smiling in his good-natured way. He worked for the British Israelite movement and had an impressive literal understanding of the Bible. There would normally be about fourteen people in the room including Antony the visionary artist who ran this 'Followers of the Way' mystery school.

Antony Bates was a wonderful teacher. He was always at his best when talking off the cuff, responding to a question. For example when answering a question about the origin of the mystery teachings he would take one back in time to about 3000 BC to explain how the Ancient Hebrews were the most holy people on the planet and were thus trusted with our planets' solar history and sacred mystery teachings.

In time, the Ancient Hebrews taught the Jews some of the ancient mysteries that eventually became the source of the Torah. Beautiful divine terminology such as, 'Jerusalem', 'Galilee' and 'Bethlehem' were materialised and used to describe physical cities, lakes and towns but originally these terms had a more sacred spiritual meaning.[7]

Antony described the Old Testament as being in part the soul history of our planet but many spiritual analogies have been personified by the Jews to describe their own race's struggle to survive. For instance, the astonishing story of the Jews' escape from slavery in Egypt, when pursued by the furious Pharaoh, who promptly lost his men when the Red Sea separated allowing the Jews to escape but then engulfed the Egyptians, was a reworking of a tragic story from the 'Fall' when the whole planet was deluged by water.

Antony would pass onto us Mr Ferrier's information about how the Master, commonly known as Jesus, Christ, the Lord was not born as 'Jesus' at all, as indeed Siddhartha was not born as The Buddha. 'Jesus' was his initiate name, a state of being that we can all achieve if we live a loving and compassionate life. His real name was Ioannes, or 'John' (its westernised interpretation). There was no virgin birth and there was no literal resurrection, for we were taught that 'Jesus' was taken down from the cross and hidden away in the Syrian hills by his followers.[8]

I was curious about these biblical story explanations but what really appealed to me was Todd Ferrier's vision of our spiritual planet before its fall into matter more than four and a half billion years ago; how Lucifer was deceived into altering our gravity on the seventh plane of our celestial sphere and ever since has been castigated as the great betrayer of mankind.

Back in the care home Penny's mum explains how her daughter will be getting married as soon as she can find a flat to rent.

"She'll be lucky. My Charlie's been looking for a place for over a year and 'e ain't found a place yet."

"Where 'bouts does 'e want to live then?"

"Dunno. Anywhere really, so long as it's not too far away. I would 'ate that ya know, if 'e were too far away. 'E said somefing about living in Brockley. That would be nice that would. Mind you there aren't many whites living there now. P'r'aps 'e would be better off living in Catford. I like it there."

"So 'andy for the shops."

"Yeah."

"Well I'll ask my Patrick for you. I'm not promising anything mind, not promising. But he knows of someone, who knows of one of them whatdoyercallits… er, oh yes, estate agents. You've got to be in the know, you know. It's the only way to get a place these days."

"So expensive too."

"Yeah, ever so 'spensive."

"Why I remember when it was easy to get a place, like. Just kept an eye out on the boards and then applied. 'Twas easy. None of this 'ere references lark. Just a week's money in advance."

"Yeah."

"But you 'ave to foller every bit of hope. Go after everything."

"I am. Me and Penny went to one of those owsyerfather agents the other day and they wanted landlord references, bankers' references… I ain't even in a bloody bank!"

"My granddaughter…"

"The bugger wouldn't even take my phone number. Now I know those lazy baskets can't be bothered to write. They just pick up the phone… No thanks dear I'm slimmin'."

"But my granddaughter got a flat easy. Just goes to show, don't it. It's just luck."

"Eh? How?"

"A friend gave it to her, like. She didn't 'ave t' look 'ardly."

"I dunno. I pay sixpence a week for these teabags. Everyone makes rude remarks about my tea."

◆

Black clad Mrs Dowding hung in the shadows like a crow trapped in the vestry. A white coat beamed at her. "Come now Louisa my dear. Your dinner's getting cold on the table. You don't want the matron to come down here now, do you?"

"I couldn't care less about the fuckin' old matron, an' I hate you an' all. I can't eat the food. They can't cook for toffee. I hate it when they all stare at me in that dining room."

Two more white coats appeared, too many for Louisa to handle so she rose up and flew away down the corridor.

In the staff room Iris sought help whilst filling in an application form.

"How do you spell welfare?"

"Welfare what?"

"Department."

"W-E-L-F-A-R-E..."

"'Ang on."

"Where are ya up to?"

"F."

"Right... A-R-E. Now... D-E-P-A-R-T-M-E-N-T. Got it?"

"Yep. Right. Name and address?"

"Well, if she don't know by now..."

"Where was I born?"

"Cor blimey!"

"I would keep it a secret if I were you!"

"Haa..nnnah!"

"Shut up you lot. Bleedin' 'ell. They don't 'arf want to know a lot aboutcha."

"They don't want to know about that do they?"

"She can't remember the first time, she were blind drunk!"

"No I weren't! I'll have you know I was a virgin on me wedding day!"

"Oh yeah love, sure."

"Rotten lot. What's the phone number here?"

"Get up and have a look."

"Balls."

"Er... it's 857****."

"Present post?"

"Should know that by now. Care attendant. Class two aren't you?"

"I've been in this hole for two years now."

"There you are then. Grade two. I'm a grade one you know. I've been here the longest."

"I've been on the council for forty years!"

"Jean's only grade three."

"What people do we look after?"

"Geriatric."

"She can't spell that!"

"I can spell the jerry you put under the bed!"

"Yeah."

"Experience?"

"Plenty of that."

"Haa..nnnah."

"None!"

"What about all those years you've been at it?"
"Qualifications? Oh gawd. None of them."
"Left school at fourteen didn't cha?"
"I've got all the qualifications that I need!"
"Tea dear."
"Ta. 'Ere, does the forenames mean the first names... don't it?"
"Yeah. It's the Christian names isn't it?"
"Yeah. Like John. Not your afters name like."
"Here. Time we were back."
"Yeah."

In my own strange individualistic way I had always been a seeker, wondering why I had been born and for what purpose and early in life had been fobbed off with all sorts of unsatisfying data, such as: the biblical concept of the world being created in seven days, or the scientific big bang theory, insinuating that everything was an accident and that there was no intelligent creation of life at all.

In time I read, or gleaned from Antony, that celestial angels created embryonic human beings from the Elohim that encompassed our planet as it swam in the divine circulus in the un-fallen days, before the tragic fall of our planet into matter. This was our soul history. This was how we all began.

Our tiny embryonic soul always commenced life in the spiritual vegetable, or flower kingdom and would gradually incarnate through the beautiful flowers and trees until one wonderful day it would metamorphose into the pure creature kingdom and again experience life incarnating in the loving creatures, forever moving slowly inwards and upwards, until it was finally ready to transform into a spiritual human form.[9]

Once in human form our soul continued its long journey, aspiring to travel through twelve human degrees of consciousness, passing through angelic and then celestial stages of development until it finally reached the outer divine realm. This process of evolution took untold ages (probably many millions of years) but in heaven time is not a factor. But sadly, since the fall, all human creation has been suspended, which means that we are all, at soul, at least as old as our materialised planet; over five billion years of age!

Behind the locked door old Samuel tries to remember where he is.

"I don't know where I am. Why am I here? Don't I have a home to go to? I used to go out a lot through that door... but they don't let me go out alone anymore. I'm not sure why. They might think I will get lost but I am already lost. You would think they would allow me a little bit of freedom.

"I don't know who I am. I used to know. I was certain then. I did all the usual things, went to school. Had a job, went out with a girl… well I think I did. They tell me I got married but I can't remember her name. A woman comes to visit me sometimes. They say she is my wife. She looks familiar. She sits with me and we go into the garden. She talks all the time. I do know her voice but I can never remember what she says. I just nod and smile. It is nice to have a visitor but this woman always cries and then she goes away again.

"Most days I just sit in my chair and look at the faces around me. I don't know any of their names. They seem to watch the television but it means nothing to me, just noise. I prefer to sit in the quiet. I like my mealtimes but can never remember if I have eaten or not, or if I am about to have my breakfast or dinner. I live for my cup of tea. You have to live for something."

The moon is alive. She watches us closely influencing our actions. She came all those ages ago to save us, to re-energise our fallen planet, Judah, our wasteland. Then Luna shone like the goddess she truly is and fed us her light and sub-atomic particles and allowed us to sup from her waters but as we awoke from our deathly slumber we greedily demanded more from our saviour. Instead of releasing her from her tender loving embrace and gratefully thanking her for her kind sacrifice, we raped Luna. We betrayed the trust she gave us. We trashed her, sucked all the life out of her, wallowed in her luxurious waters and flung her into our eternal orbit, like a neglected broken doll. Even today we enslave Luna's lower life forms and relish eating their flesh.[10]

He lay upon his bed, almost finished, yet he mustered enough vitality in an effort to revise his worthier deeds, wary of a final confrontation by an awkward angel looking at his mortal balance sheet. Anguished he pondered what good had he done? Had he done anything useful at all?

He repeatedly gasped but when his final breath had gone he felt warm instead of cold and joyous instead of fearful. His aches and pain just vanished and all worries were swept away. He laughed at his foolish fears and wanted to roll about his bed in ecstasy but then he became aware of her presence.

Beautiful with her colours, aroma and radiance she descended and caressed him, effortlessly raising him up into a spiritual embrace. His soul connected with this fabulous divine energy; he was no longer his boring self but at one with an illuminated being, who could make sense of his past, present and future.

Time passed on by as he relived his childhood, his formative years and his adulthood. He wept at all the missed opportunities to bring genuine love into the world. Then at the right moment she directed his shades towards the astral, occult planes and guided his soul upon its way.

Gratified the husk grinned as it was buried without much ceremony. A grave digger covered the garbage with earth.

Three genial old ladies swept along the corridor. Elegant Evelyn Saunders led the trio, clutching Joan's hand with Joyce clinging on at the back of the group, with her brown handbag dragging along the floor. The ladies looked so pleased with themselves.

"Where are you going Eve?"

"Oh we're going to school now," replied Eve as she led her giggling friends further up the corridor.

"Hello dear."

"Hello Rose."

"I'm not Rose, I'm Iris. But you got yer flowers right, didn't cha!'

Sometimes we meet people for the first time who seem incredibly familiar. It is as if they have been close to us in a previous life but not all such experiences are good. I remember the way he looked at me, this oppressor of mankind. I should have been safe in the Order's sanctuary but he stood in the doorway blocking my escape and I felt the hair on my neck stand up as my blood ran cold.

Smiling he started to scrutinise me. His eyes bore through me as I tried to answer his searching questions. I could not return his gaze and looked helplessly beyond him into the vestry, hoping for someone to rescue me but no-one came. It was as if his ancient antennae had tuned into me, probing, reading, sifting through my strengths and weaknesses, analysing anything that I might have to say.

I would have liked to have bustled past him, full of gusto but instead I withdrew into my own insurmountable little refuge, leaving behind a few stammering words, a fool's gift to its master. But I knew I could not trick him. He left me with a sigh, disappointed with the fruits of his labours. His words reverberated around my head. It would take me days to recover from his strange verbal or psychic assault and I wondered if I had fallen under the spell of this dark soul in a previous incarnation.

FOUR

College, Education and Dietary Changes

O NE DAY IN the mid-seventies, I was preparing food in my mother's kitchen, planning to make an omelette. I fetched an egg or two out of the fridge but when it came to cracking the eggs I hesitated for a moment and thought about the little life within the egg that had already been sacrificed for my meal. I decided it was unnecessary for me to eat eggs, that I could do without them. That same day I also gave up milk and cheese and thus set out on my long voyage as a vegan, or quasi-vegan as I would occasionally weaken and eat chocolate or ice cream.

Later I would submit articles for Vegan Views and met Malcolm the austere editor in his Wray Crescent vegan house. Malcolm had an intellectual slant on the world and would query my poorly developed spiritual ramblings but we had a lot in common so he was a good friend to discuss relevant current issues.

Wray Crescent was always lively, with hippy characters present like Catweazle, who was an excellent vegan baker, Majoike a fierce Dutch girl and an array of interesting visitors, like Roger who wore a kaftan and later lived like a holy man on Crete.

Near the VV publication date, I would offer to help prepare the magazine but in reality probably got in the way. Malcolm could not tolerate poorly written submissions and would rewrite nearly all the offerings, including mine. A fruitarian who called himself, Charlight Utang would send in beautiful pages, glistening in colour, with letters and words strewn about the page but It was always a struggle to make sense of his articles that were probably written on an acid high.

I went to meet Charlight who lived at his parents' house in Kew. His real name was Charles but when he studied orangutangs at university he decided to call himself Charlight Utang because they did not have anyone using the 'U' section of the university letter boxes. At that time Charlight was a budding shaman and would literally go into the Indonesian jungle to study with holy men. He lived on fruit and being a neuro-biologist knew about the metabolism of fruit in great detail. Indeed his room was overflowing with plants with an abundance of avocado plants and pineapples reaching up to the ceiling.

In time, Charlight became quite a celebrity in Kew, frequently changing his name before settling on Jungleyes Love. He opened a crystal shop in Kew called, 'World Tree Mend Us'. He famously received a commission from a customer who wanted him to design a pendulum that would enable him to win on the horses. The first time it was used, the pendulum won the owner £800 but on its second attempt it refused to swing so the pendulum was returned with instructions to replace the silver parts with gold. Charlight reputedly added a relic of horse bone to the pendulum. The next time it was used at the Cheltenham Gold Cup. The pendulum indicated a sure winner. The owner bet all his £800 on the horse indicated and he duly won £33,000![11]

My exam results arrived and I opened the letter with trepidation. I found I had done well enough to be accepted at Bretton Hall, a teacher training college in Yorkshire, to study English/Drama.[12] This was my big opportunity to educate myself as I had completely shot myself in the foot at secondary school.

At college I enjoyed the Sociology and Psychology and loved the English Literature but found the Drama hard going as it took a great effort from me to memorise my lines.

I met Carol on the outskirts of our college, waiting for her bus on a lonely country road. She wore an artist's smock and wore her hair in pigtails. With her dark hair and tanned face she looked every inch like a native American squaw. Never comfortable with small talk I wafted my hand towards some cows grazing in a distant field and told her that they contained the lower souls of Venus and muttered something about it being quite wrong to eat them. The squaw smiled but didn't say too much, probably thought I should be sectioned.

A week later we were walking around Bretton's beautiful lake, hand in hand, inseparable now except for an unremitting squabble about religion. Later she showed me a portrait that she had drawn of me the previous year, during her psychic period. She said that although I thought I had found her, she had really manifested me!

Carol told me about her childhood that had initially been difficult as her elders had warred amongst each other:

Hilda was bullied and bashed by her aggressive spouse
and the other men in her unhappy house.
Nevertheless she did her best to cleanse and
calm her home of its internal sufferings.
In the end she quickly passed;
Dropsy they said.
She was barely fifty years of age.
So then this sibylline sought revenge on these selfish men,
By displaying her decomposing corpse at the top of the stairs,

On a little ledge, like an open coffin.
But none of the warring men had the etheric eyes to see;
Just little Carol whose dreams were disturbed for an eternity.

Carol and I used to attend all kinds of spiritual groups in South Yorkshire. We liked the open-minded Quakers and checked out the vegetarian communities in the Dales but it seemed to us that most of the spiritual action was occurring in Leeds. When I became the secretary of the Bretton Hall Philosophical Society I invited the Hare Krishna group to attend a meeting at college. They spent all day dancing and chanting around the college, in and out of the library and dining halls, and I met some of their remarkable characters.

It was not easy to be a brahmcharya in Yorkshire but Vikram was determined to press ahead with his desire to become first a sannyasin and then a yogi. He had no family ties having been denounced as, 'Beyond weird' by his father and auntie.

His first influence was with the orange-robed Hare Krishna group that would parade around Leeds, chanting and dancing. He spent nearly a year with them and through the devotees he learnt the ideals of ahimsa: non-violence in words or action and he became a vegetarian. When he changed his name from Billy to Vikram, shaved off all his hair and practised chanting Hare Krishna and

Om all day long, his father finally flipped and he was slung out of his family home.

It was a chance glance through his local paper that led Vikram onto the next stage of his spiritual journey. He had been looking at the small ads, to find somewhere impossibly cheap to live, when he noticed a yoga class being set up at the other end of town. This appealed to him as doing yoga exercises would fit in perfectly with his meditative lifestyle, so on the given day he set off on his bicycle and rode to the meditation centre where the yoga class began. But when he arrived at the Yoga Centre he found all the classes exceedingly expensive to join so he sat on the steps outside and silently meditated for spiritual direction.

Eventually a kindhearted student girl sat down to speak with him and gave him the name of her brother, whom she said was similar to Vikram. Following this lead Vikram set off to meet Suresh, who regularly played the sitar at one of the Hindu temples. In time Suresh became his close companion and joined Vikram in his Vedic studies with the elders of the Hindu Temple.

Vikram had no difficulty with the vow of celibacy but Suresh always struggled with his emotions and after completing his university training accepted an arranged marriage with a beautiful local Hindu girl. After this Vikram wandered between different eastern religious factions, always favouring the Hindu tradition but he still loved the sheer exuberance of the Hare Krishna fraternity and the broad openness of the Buddhist community.

One of the factors that Vikram struggled to understand was the concept of the soul. He understood the position of the Buddhists, who denied the soul, and the Brahmin who said that Atman was vital to one's being so, representing his Leeds temple, he took the opportunity to travel to a conference in London to listen to three sages who were discussing this very subject.

On the day of the conference the Hindu guru began the proceedings by stating that atman entailed the concept of the self as a spiritual rather than physical being. Thus it was important to emphasise detachment from the material world and whenever possible to practice asceticism. He said that in this world it could be argued that the spiritual being (the atman) has a human experience rather than the human being having a spiritual experience. Thus the atman is the immortal aspect of our mortal existence with the individual self hidden in every object of creation including humankind.

He explained how atman is Brahmin and how the microcosm which represents the macrocosm in each of us, imparts to us divine qualities and possibilities and provides us with consciousness and the reason to exist and to experience the pain and pleasure of earthly life.

'The Self' is the silent partner in all our deeds and experiences. It is the observer and the indweller of all embodied beings. You cannot describe 'The Self' in human language, as it is beyond the senses and the mind. "There the eyes cannot travel, nor speech nor mind. Nor do we know how to explain it to the disciples. It is other than the known and beyond the unknown."

'The Self' can only be experienced when all sensory activity ceases and the mind is freed from all thoughts and sense objects and from the torment of desires, which are the main cause of all human activity and suffering. When the mind subsides into quietude the experience of 'The Self' arises into the beautiful state of Oneness.

The guru further explained the importance of Dharma with the universals that govern life and illustrated the concept of personal sva-dharma by stories from the Bhagavad Gita.

The Buddhist teacher was the next to speak, an accomplished American who played with his mali-beads as he discussed the Buddhist notion of soul theory. He said there are three kinds of teachers in the world. The first teacher taught the existence of an eternal ego-entity that outlasts death. He is called the eternalist. The second teacher teaches a temporary ego-entity which becomes annihilated at death: He is the materialist. The third teacher teaches neither an eternal nor a temporary ego-entity. He is the Buddha.

The Buddha taught that what we call ego, self, soul, personality, etc., are merely conventional terms that do not refer to any real, independent entity. There is no reason to believe that there is an eternal soul that comes from heaven or that is created by itself and that will transmigrate or proceed straight away either to heaven or hell after death.

The teacher said that Buddhists are likely to state that no man has produced anything to promote mankind by postulating a soul and its imaginary working. Searching for a soul in man is like searching for something in a dark empty room. But the poor man will never realise that what he is searching for is not in the room. It is very difficult to make such a person understand the futility of his search.

Those who believe in the existence of a soul are not in a position to explain what and where it is. The Buddha's advice is not to waste our time over this unnecessary speculation and devote our time to strive for our salvation. When we have attained perfection then we will be able to realise whether there is a soul or not.

The American went on to explain in some detail the four noble truths and the eightfold path which is the root of Buddhism.

The final teacher was a Christian mystic. His words can be recapitulated as follows: Man himself is like a beautiful amulet with its various sections, each one more precious than the other. The outer man, or physical form, is only the outer case which contains the precious stone. The mind, or lower man, is only the inner case. The higher mind is the place where the gem is resting. The soul is the gem itself. But the spirit is not the gem in its form or colour: it is much more: it is its light. (13)

This elderly man also spoke of the importance of ahimsa but called it the path to purity. He was also against cruelty to animals and said that many creatures had once been on the human plane and that it was both wrong and evil for science to exploit them.

All the speakers entranced Vikram but he was not really any closer to selecting his chosen notion of atman/soul. But he was even more determined to follow his spiritual path, to first become a sannyasin and then perhaps one day he would become a teacher of the 'vedas'.

At twenty-four I was one of the oldest students in my year at Bretton Hall. My college pals were somewhat bemused to see me drinking blackcurrant juice at the college bar, which cost 2p a pint but I was determined to manage my grant properly and not run up a debt. In fact, with my ongoing vocational job in the old people's home, Carol and I saved enough money to spend the summer in Greece.

We flew to Athens and then went by ferry boat to Rhodes, Kos, Patmos, Lipsi and Mykinos, usually sleeping for free on the beaches, sometimes illicitly using the Red Cross facilities to shower. On our £1 a day allowance we generally survived on bread and salad, maybe having a cooked meal, like stuffed pepper and rice, in the evenings at a taverna. They were blissful days. The Greeks were so wonderful and kind and the sea was just magnificent. It was as if we were in Utopia!

Back at Bretton I was bemused that we English students mainly read and discussed books, analysing them to death but were not required to do much creative writing. The exception being on one occasion we were asked to write a children's story; mine was about a randy hedgehog. Fellow student Clair wrote about her rabbits:

Clair's rabbits are loving and gentle.
Clair's rabbits are loving and kind.
You can see them in her picture book,
She created them with her sentient mind.

So in my last term I wrote a play called, 'Twenty Minutes Meditation'. My colleagues and friends performed it for me. The general idea was to indicate how hard it is to rise above the lower mind during a meditation. In retrospect I should have called the play, 'Twenty Minutes of Crappy Thinking' or something like that. Bill, very much a free spirit, took on the role as the meditator and looked suitably impressive. I learnt the hard way that writing a play is far more difficult than it appears, although my tutors who watched the play were gently encouraging.

Twenty Minutes Meditation – Will Change the Face of Society
> (Misquote by Mahrishi Maresh Yogi)

SCENE:

The record 'Govinda' is playing. 'Richard' lights some incense, takes the record off and sits cross-legged on the floor with his fingers encircled.

ALL VOICES: Chanting 'Om' and then 'Ahimsa' (for one minute).

VOICE 1:   Shilton, Keegan and Case. No. Clemence in goal. The Villa fullback, whatshisname? Gidman. Todd and Beattie with Mills as the other full back. Give Talbot a try. Who the hell can go in midfield? Francis or Watkins? No. Greenhoff, I suppose. Brooking is definitely in. Then Keegan and Mariner, with any in-form left winger. Leave Channon on the subs bench.

VOICE 2:   Come on now. Stop this bloody rubbish. Om Ahimsa.

VOICE 1:   It's alright. Nobody will know. You can take it. It's not stealing.

VOICE 4:   After all it was over two years ago.

VOICE 1:   You're entitled to it. You paid a quarter of the deposit so you may as well collect it all.

VOICE 4:   Twenty pounds! What a little windfall!

VOICE 1:   The others will have long forgotten. They don't care. It's all yours. Take it. Why should they suddenly remember the old electricity deposit?

VOICE 4:   You took the responsibility.

VOICE 1:   Take it. You deserve the money.

VOICE 4:   No-one will ever know.

VOICE 2:   Om. Ahimsa

ALL VOICES: Om Ahimsa (repeat for twenty seconds).

VOICE 3:   Here she is again. Her face emanating a
            sensitive feeling of exquisiteness. Long
            hair swept down, as though to her toes.
            Perhaps it should never end, this ever-
            flowing form of beauty. And her eyes,
            so full of dark secrets, alas they are
            hurt and pretend to come alive when
            really they are shrouded by tears. I wish
            she would not pretend. When will she
            learn to trust again? Am I supposed to
            bring you alive? I love to touch you.
            It is as though I can feel the sweetest
            music. When you move you flow like
            waves and I watch as though transfixed
            by this eternal source of feeling.
            Sometimes I can see you in the trees.
            You are the magnolia which causes the
            leaves to grow. I wonder if I stared at
            you for long enough whether I could
            perceive your dryad form. I want to
            take you upon the water. We could go
            rowing together across the lake, isolated
            by some apparent freak of nature to
            spend precious seconds together in
            this vast stretch of time. Why do you
            mock me so? Why do you doubt me?
            Of course I want to love you physically.
            To hold you naked in my arms. To pin
            you down. But far more important is
            this mystery of your being which has

spun its eternal web about me. I must understand, otherwise I shall certainly die, for my aspirations will quickly fall and then, what is there left to live for?

MUSIC: Debussy flute music for approximately two minutes.

VOICES: Om Ahimsa (for approx. twenty seconds).

VOICE 2: It annoys me so much. When the pipes get blocked up they call for a plumber. A window breaks and a glazier gets called in. When the telly doesn't work, the TV repair man gets called for and so on. No-one takes responsibility for their own lives any more.

VOICE 4: But they do. They work hard for, say, forty hours a week and earn the right to pay for things to be fixed for them. You can't expect them to work all day and then return home to do all these tricky time-consuming tasks. It would be too much of a strain.

VOICE 2: You miss my point. By the very lives we lead we become over specialised in totally inappropriate areas of experience. We are socialised to rely on other people to do things for us. Money being the deciding factor. Now what is going to happen when our technological society starts to break down? When our power sources, such as oil, gas and electricity begin to dry up? Can you imagine the panic when twenty million people go to plug something into their power socket and nothing happens? The majority of them will be totally impotent in this situation.

VOICE 4: It's too farcical. At any rate people are adaptable. The last world war proved that.

VOICE 2: Yes but our dependence upon technology has risen greatly since then. It is the ignorant manner by which we are veering away from a natural and healthy way of living which bothers me. People sleepwalk their way through their lives. They are totally trusting. They do not want to think too deeply about society. They would rather follow the given pattern and apart from the occasional grumble, always do what they are told by our inconspicuous but sinister figures in power. The trouble is they are following such a false way of living that all natural instincts will soon be left behind and then faced by some future disaster their only solution will be to commit mass suicide.

ALL THREE VOICES TALKING AT THE SAME TIME:

VOICE 1:   You don't understand people very well because their area of experience is so different from yours. They want to be happy, whatever that means. They desire to be liked, loved and accepted and be comfortable in the most bourgeois sense of the word. They want to find themselves a rut and progress along it to make it as comfortable as they can and then when they become bored they want to be free of it. So some people climb out of their rut and promptly fall into another one and follow the same pattern, a little game called stagnation. Surprisingly the most stagnant people of all are often the most highly regarded; maybe for having persevered with a loveless marriage so that one anniversary they can say, "Oh we have been married for forty years!" And everyone considers that is a wonderful achievement even though you know they cannot stand the sight of each other. Or someone else might proudly remark, "I've worked for the same firm for twenty-five years," expecting and often getting heartfelt congratulations even though they have previously revealed to you that they are bored senseless by the work they do. Programmes like Crossroads and Coronation Street teach the masses how to persevere with their boring lives as a kind of template, the telly being the shrine.

VOICE 2: It is crazy the way prices keep going up. It doesn't make sense at all. Why, a few months ago a quarter of tea cost 22p. Now it costs 32p and they say it will be 40p soon. It is a real liberty! We are bred on a nice cup of tea and now they take advantage of us. What will the pensioners say? What will they do if they are unable to afford a cup of tea? There will be millions of bad tempered old folk suffering from tannin withdrawal symptoms, Clinics and surgeries will be overrun by trying to deal with them. Dandelion coffee could become the rage with everyone cultivating the dandelion root in their back garden. Overnight Britain could become a nation of herbal tea brewers!

VOICE 3: My girlfriend doesn't see me anymore. She has her own vision of me resembling Warren Beatty, or when she feels like being ravaged, Steve McQueen. She always closes her eyes when we kiss. I used to be carefree and sloppy. I was a mess when it came to clothes. When we met she gave me a long hard look. I thought, 'This is it! She fancies me.' In fact she was already mentally changing my clothes and grooming my hair. I would do. I had a certain potential. Several months later I only faintly resemble my old self. I am now a neat cardboard cutout man. True my jacket does not quite fit and my hair sticks up at the back but I keep her happy. Her friends do not turn away in revulsion when they meet me. She has also changed my name. I am no longer 'Dick' but 'Ricky' or sometimes 'Rich' and she introduces me as a poet. (whisper) Whereas I am really a hospital porter. We meet twice a week and at weekends we lose ourselves in a kind of social whirl. I don't like it very much but she does. She is an action girl. Everyone pretends to be what they are not, even me. It becomes embarrassing when they ask to see my poetry. They all have so much to say, chatting endlessly about their books and films, glorifying any little thing that they have done. Holidays are the thing of the moment. It gets quite exciting listening to them talk; The Costa Del Sol; Tunisia; St Tropez.

When they ask me where I am going on my vacation I tell them that I am going to Ramsgate to stay with my Nan.

VOICE 4: Mark, I think I understand what is meant by 'vision' now. It need not be a visual picture inside the head at all, such as William Blake's work implies. Rather it is an intense feeling, or motion, whereby you feel very deeply about something. It becomes a tremendous passion. Thus the anti-vivisectionists have their vision of man working in harmony with the animal kingdom instead of torturing and abusing them. If the vision, or motion within them becomes so strong and clear they get up off their backsides and do something about it. So many people are visionaries but don't recognise it because the mind does not picture their feelings. Really it is quite easy to visualise our ideals but we don't usually think in these terms when we are inspired. We just are! I always thought that Blake woke up one morning with a wonderful picture in his head and then rushed into his studio and used his skill to paint it. More likely he felt a tremendous motion and being an artist was able to picture these feelings using his Druid folklore and love of mythology to find the appropriate symbols. It might go deeper than that of course. His wonderful painting of the un-fallen Lucifer has always moved me. Perhaps Blake was Lucifer himself and could thus intensely feel the angel's beauty in the unfallen days.

ALL VOICES: Om Ahimsa (chant for twenty seconds)

VOICE 1: Who am I?

VOICE 2: Who am I?

VOICE 3: Who am I?

VOICE 4: Who am I?

ALL VOICES: Who am I? (silence for five seconds)

VOICE 1: You're a silly little twerp, that's what you are. Sitting cross-legged on the floor. You big pseudo. What are you trying to do anyway? Find Peace? (laughter) Happiness? Love? (snigger) Fine chance you have with all those stupid thoughts. You will be better off getting up and doing something. Come on. Stop wasting time. (Slight pause)

VOICE 2: Who am I? (Silence for five seconds)

VOICE 4: You are Richard, hospital porter, bogus poet, bogus everything. Kind-hearted, mild mannered, unassertive, easy going and easily led. Five foot eight, somewhat lustful – that is when you get the chance! Loyal, scared, warm yet hard. Romantic, a dim wit, rather spiritual, rather pathetic. You have anarchist tendencies, a socialist perhaps. You are a loser. People cannot relate to you. You must change. Be assertive. Find your own centre.

VOICE 2: Who am I? (pause for five seconds)

VOICE 3: When the time is right you may learn who you really are. Your soul is as old as the world itself and contains so much grief and travail that only if it is imperative for you to know will your soul be opened up for you to see and understand. We are all heavily veiled. It is for our own protection. But this is the age of the return. Those who caused the fall of this world must now return and lead us back again. It is the truest form of karma. We must pass through all the difficult stages which once led to our fall into matter. As you return you will remember the highest ideals and know who you really are.

ALL VOICES: Death to the monarchy. Trample Princess Anne under a mass of stampeding horses. Have Prince Charles neutered by a pack of blonde giggling girls. Remove Prince Phillip's vocal chords by choking his inevitable tie around his neck. Lock Queen

Elizabeth into a cell covered by pictures of herself. Send the two younger princes into any London Comprehensive school. Ship Margaret out to sea on a barge overloaded with pink gin. May all the hangers on do a day's work in any chemical factory. Give the land to the people, to those who need it the most, or to people who will put the land to the best use. Pour the monarch's wealth into natural technology projects such as energy from the waves, solar power. Now, as for the church…

ALL VOICES: Om

VOICE 4:   (singing and playing his guitar)
Ah he's falling in love with Beatrice again.
She's the symbol of beauty in his vision.
She's the loveliest lady he has ever seen.
She's a true Madonna from his dreams.
But what can the poor boy do?
For his love, it's impossible.
For she is a saint, ah she's a nun
And he is just a lowly man.
But he's falling in love with Beatrice again.
She's a symbol of beauty in his vision.
(Guitar play – then repeat)

An alarm clock indicated the end of twenty minutes' meditation.

Like all my fellow students, in my final term of college I started filling out application forms for teaching posts. I was prepared to go anywhere in the south of England and applied for primary and secondary school placements. This being the mid-seventies, teaching posts were hard to obtain, no matter how good your college distinctions. After about fifty applications my concentration started to deviate and I became focused on the form particulars. For my age I figured out I had lived for approximately 832,896,000 seconds, bar the odd leap year. Being of a practical nature I divided the number by four to get the approximate number of breaths that I had taken in my life so far: 208,224,000. So more than two hundred and eight million gasps of air: that was a lot of oxygen!

My new-fangled application form must have created interest because I was invited to two interviews; one, teaching Humanities in a secondary school in Maidstone and the other for a special school, also in Kent. I took the special school position because I preferred to class teach. I was also quite intrigued by the headteacher who spent most of my interview talking about himself and how he had been offered the post of headteacher as a reward for his war heroics.

So, in September 1977, still heavily influenced by Charlight, I became the only fruitarian teacher in Kent, probably the UK. The school children were defined as, 'Educationally sub normal'. It was such a cruel definition, for these days all of the children that I taught then would be in a mainstream school and some would fare quite well for themselves in life beyond school.[(14)]

Like all new teachers I had to learn to tread the path between being friendly and assertive, otherwise I would be rendered ineffective. Running the school sports teams gave me kudos with the older boys as I taught them to play football and cricket. I would lift their fitness by making them run and run, often leading them from the front. Our football team became quite good but I would sometimes have to sit on our star player Mark when he had a meltdown. The game would then proceed with me refereeing the game still squatting on the back of this raging child. Of course you would never recourse to such an action these days but I knew that Mark's temper was usually short-lived and besides he was my star player, so I did not want to send him off!

To my eternal surprise I found that I could teach children to read and write by focusing in on their individual learning patterns. I would discern their learning block and gently ease their way through it. It was almost a psychic teaching process, sort of teaching them to think. Of course most of the time I would class teach by using traditional methods. I was fortunate to be at such a well-run special school and worked hard to emulate the excellent teachers. It was the start of my career in special education.

I switched schools in 1980 to teach at The Vale School in Haringey.[15] It was a school for physically handicapped children. I spent the first two weeks in shock because I had never been in close contact with children with disabilities before and was emotionally traumatised by the children in my care.

In my class of twelve children, all packed into a tiny classroom, I had an assortment of cerebral palsy, two boys with muscular dystrophy, a tiny boy with a congenital condition akin to thalidomide, a girl with one arm, hydrocephalus, a boy who could only speak on his in-drawing breath and a lad with mild scoliosis who really ought to have been in the local comprehensive. In fact all of them should have been in mainstream education but curiously in those days parents usually opted for the loving security of the special school.

For my first two weeks at The Vale I taught like a robot. Then I gradually broke through my emotional malaise and started to see my class as children with a broad range of ability and needs instead of being 'handicapped'. I can still recall all their names today by visualising them sitting at their classroom desks.

After I had been on a series of specialised AA swimming and sports courses Marjorie, our lovely sunny headteacher, wanted me to become the school sports coach. I tried it for a year but missed the theatre and interaction of the classroom. I did enjoy teaching the children to swim and one year our school won the Inner London Gala for disabled children.

The staff would all play jokes on each other. One winter's day I was in the swimming pool teaching Andrew when the fire alarm went off. This was curious because we were always forewarned when fire drill was due. Also odd, my Teaching Assistant was missing! I managed to haul Andrew out of the water and helped to dry him with the huge towels. I half dried myself and put on a white towelling dressing-gown. I dressed Andrew as fast as I could, bundled him into a wheelchair and ushered him out of the fire doors into the playground. My hair was dripping wet and I wore flip flops on my feet in the snow. The whole school were lined up in the playground and there was Marjorie and the teachers all grinning and laughing at me as I trudged towards them half naked in the snow.

The Vale School was literally in the shadow of the giant Rowntree's fruit gum factory so we always had the fruit gum smell pervading the school. One year Rowntree's had a refit and Princess Anne came to reopen the factory. I gathered my class of children on the street in the pouring rain to greet the Princess Royal. We had made a, 'Welcome Princess Anne' banner and had little Union Jack flags to wave. The huge limousine turned up ten minutes late and parked right in front of my drenched bunch of kids. A flunkey held a huge umbrella over the Princess as she stepped out of her car and she made a beeline for us. She was all smiles and thanked the children for coming out in the rain to greet her. Then she turned to me and hissed, "For goodness sake get these poor children out of this rain," and then stomped into the factory with the sparse crowd cheering her every step.

It was not always fun at The Vale. In the summer term of my first year, Angela, who had hydrocephalus with a shunt to control the fluids in her brain, died after a terrible stroke. I represented the school at her funeral in Tooting. I had never been to a funeral before and was the only white face amongst hundreds of mourners in the cemetery, many up from the Caribbean. From a distance I watched the coffin being slowly dropped into the grave with tears streaming from my eyes.

The huge crowd sang gospel hymns and rejoiced in Angela's life. It was a stirring and moving occasion. Later I went back to the family's modern flat in Tottenham. The parents treated me like a Lord but I could barely speak. All I could see in front of me was Angela's pensive face as she struggled with her sums.

I stayed at the school for six years and completed a course of programmed learning, which is today called precision teaching. This detailed style of teaching really suited me and I became very confident that I could teach anyone to read and write by following this forensic approach to teaching.

By 1986 integration was the buzz word in education and we finally started to include our pupils, part-time, into the local comprehensive. I remember observing Nigel and Roy, our two delightful Duchenne's pupils. The idea was for them to mix with their able-bodied peers but they stuck together like glue in the playground, barely speaking to anyone else. In retrospect, it was probably the reverse of my own emotional trauma when I started at The Vale.

FIVE

Marriage, Birth and the Paranormal

IN THE 80S it was all the rage to go to therapy groups to try to sort out one's inner demons. John Lennon had recommended Primal Therapy via 'The Primal Scream', so I gave it a try. If only it were as easy as in Janov's book![16] Usually one worked in pairs, with an experienced therapist overseeing the whole process.

I remember moribund Paul asking for a whole group initiative. He was a small intense man with sunken eyes and was apparently fixated by the occult. He had hung around the primal groups for several weeks without much participation. He had obviously decided that today would mark his debut.

We sat around on the floor in a horse-shoe shape whilst he and his ex-girlfriend faced each other, sitting on chairs. Paul positioned people around the room where he wanted them with Yvette, one of his select group, facing opposite me. The process started and the sunlight quickly disappeared from the room.

Paul seemed to go way back into time. His hypnotic voice created a dark atmosphere and the room was gradually filled by a mist that became very cold and unworldly. He appeared to be channelling a druid who seemed to be wearing a dark habit and wielding a knife. It all seemed to be an overture to a ritual slaughter, like a young virgin in ancient times being offered to the gods.

I wanted to get out but to my horror I could no longer move. I was aware of Yvette's eyes bearing down upon me. It was as if I was part of a triangle that energised this whole drama on an esoteric level. Having no control over my own physical body was terrifying.

At the vital point of the symbolic slaughter, someone tossed a cross on a chain into the middle of the room. Paul reacted violently, as if hit by an electric current. Snake-like he hissed and stared at the cross with his mad eyes bulging but the spell he had evoked was instantly broken. The atmosphere changed, the mists lifted and I could move, so I swiftly left the room without looking back.

In the kitchen people drifted in. Everyone was shocked by what they had seen. They all seemed to be saying, "What was that all about?" Only Paul knew the answer to that question but as I left the building I also withdrew from the therapy scene for good.

As someone who always aspired towards experiencing a higher spiritual consciousness I longed for angelic enlightenment but my beautiful moments of angelic bliss were almost eclipsed by the terrifying episode that preceded, when I was almost annihilated:

It started innocently enough when I lay in bed at night trying to fall asleep. I remember being restless, tossing and turning with Carol fast asleep beside me. Then came the violent images and my concern for the boxer Frank Bruno who was due to fight for a world title, but as the night wore on the atmosphere changed and I really began to fear what was approaching me.

The sounds were excruciating, as if I were being cast into the clanging pits of hell. Something seemed to crawl out of my crown chakra, a demon so foul that I shook in terror, petrified as the evil entity moved in on me. Black clad, wolf-like, it stank of offal, as if it were composed of the foulest decomposing meat, or excrement. Its eyes blazed in hatred and I knew my life was about to end, for you cannot fight such an entity. I was just frozen in terror.

And then the miracle happened. I was plucked up by an angelic form, raised on high far away from the evil form that had so threatened me. She smelt of sweet flowers, like roses so fragrant and in her grasp I ceased being a vulnerable human and became at one with this divine being. I became love and light and knew everything you could wish to know. I relaxed with the understanding that life is a long continuous flow.

But then my mind began to intervene and I started to look for specific events that might help me and so the spell was broken and I was gently returned to my physical form. How stupid of me not to dwell for longer in this beautiful angelic presence!

I rose out of bed, astonished by my experience of heaven and hell. In the bathroom I gazed at my face, with my eyes still wide apart and with my hair standing on end, the aftermath of a terrifying adventure and wondered if I was now fully free of this demon.

Not long after Carol graduated as an Osteopath/Naturopath we moved from South Hampstead to leafy Ham. Carol worked at a clinic near Shepperton and seemed to add to her alternative therapy skills every other year. Before long she was a homeopath and acupunturist, as well as a cranial osteopath and naturopath.

So who is this, channelling Panacea in the heart of her healing sanctuary? Her hands glide like wands untangling the threads of this inner fabric until she finds the cause of such pain. Then the magic begins to swirl as she casts love and light into her patient's inner world. Gradually she tends to the blocked knots that prevent the gentle ebb and flow until at last the trapped energy is released and her patient gasps in wonder, for now she is free of pain.

On the River Thames waterfront my grandmother Lily would sit on her favourite bench, smiling benignly, waiting for someone to park themselves beside her. She hoped it would not be that elderly man, the flirt. She was tired of him and all his compliments. She preferred the companionship of the sensitive elderly ladies as they wandered home along the river bank towards Surbiton, for they were relatively easy to impress. If they were religious she might even tell them about the day she left her body, when she inadvertently did some astral travelling.

She had left her dozing body behind in a chair and found herself in the spirit dimension. She had marvelled at the beauty beyond but had started to panic when she struggled to re-enter her body. After that wonderful if scary experience she felt no fear for she knew that there was life after death.

Lily loved any opportunity to describe her cruise trip around the world, listing the places she had seen in some detail. That always impressed her victims, especially when she revealed how her draughtsman son had designed his own house in Melbourne. She also enjoyed describing her expensive bungalow on the cliffs at Folkestone and how she could have bought three more after her win on the premium bonds.

To be fair, Lily was always prepared to listen to her victim's stories, which were usually based on their family issues and she would genuinely sympathise with their personal suffering but she mainly craved the spotlight on herself. Then having trumped her victim's best offering she could return to her ground floor apartment and make tea for her doting but rather frail husband.

We listened intently as Adam told us his story about his remarkable sister Lillian:

My sister was six years older than me and we used to share a room in our old house at Ladywell. I must have been about five years old when one night I woke up to find my sister Lillian listening to a beautiful lady who stood by her bedside. I remember there was a very chilly air in the room and a blue misty light shone all around her. My throat was very sore and I was feeling thirsty so I got out of bed and went to the bathroom to drink some water. When I returned the bedroom door had closed but I was unable to approach the door. I stood transfixed outside the door listening to this soft voice and watching a blue glow shining from under the door. I could not move either forwards or backwards until eventually the blue light faded away and then I stepped forward and entered the room and returned to my bed. My sister was fast asleep as if nothing had happened. In the morning I told my parents about what I had seen but Lillian just shrugged and said she could not remember anything. This incident left me in wonder and I never forgot it, but this was just the start of Lillian's strange link to the weird and wonderful.

A year later something even more extraordinary happened. One night mum and dad had gone to a meeting in the community hall leaving Lillian to look after me and so after the normal bedtime fight about brushing teeth and so forth I was finally fast asleep in bed. Lillian then woke me up and told me to get out of bed. She actually dragged me out of bed and we went into my parents' bedroom and climbed into their big bed. Lillian did not say anything but she looked frightened and then we heard this almighty crash in our bedroom next door. It was terrifying! We hid under the sheets and waited for mum and dad to return home.

When mum came home she was cross to find us in her bed and harangued us but Lillian just pointed to the room next door and stammered, "Look." Our parents were completely astonished at what had happened to our bedroom, for the ceiling and timbers had collapsed and had fallen right across my bed.

Lillian explained what had happened: She said that she had been awakened by a loud noise in her head that had told her to, "Get out of bed now!" She was then told to carry me out of the room and close the door. Was it an angel that had guided her? or was it some kind of intuitive response to danger?

The next incident happened not long after we had moved into our new house. Lillian was friendly with

Sheila, a girl who lived a few doors away, who went to the same school as her. One evening we found Sheila pacing around the back alley trying to find her black cat. She said it had been missing for almost two days. Lillian paused for a moment and then suddenly said, "Oh, I think I know where Sooty is." We all traipsed after my sister, passing over the road to the council flats nearby. She turned into where the garages were located and listened outside one of the garages and you could hear a cat mewing. Sheila went to get her dad and eventually they found out who rented the garage and rescued Sooty. Lillian just said her angel told her where to look.

At school, Lillian was always considered one of the brightest girls in her class, being particularly good at arithmetic and calculation. She enjoyed the research of her science lessons but in her fourth year she had a particularly traumatic occasion during a biology lesson. She arrived at the laboratory at the start of her lesson to find little carcasses of frogs and toads lying on petri dishes ready to be dissected by her class. Being of a sensitive nature Lillian felt a wave of revulsion running through her which seemed to trigger a seizure. She cried out aloud and then collapsed to the floor writhing around in a semi-conscious state. The Science teacher eased her onto her side and cradled her head whilst a messenger dashed off to the office to call for an ambulance. But within ten minutes Lillian had recovered her senses, announced she had no intention of cutting up the little creatures and retired to the library where she quietly read a book with tears still in her eyes.

Despite her protests Lillian was taken to the hospital where after considerable testing it was announced that she may have abnormal brainwaves that could lead to temporary epilepsy. The Doctors described this episode as an 'aura', or a partial seizure of her temporal lobe. Lillian declined taking any drugs and brushed off the whole incident saying she would have been perfectly alright if she had not been required to dissect innocent creatures. But we subsequently found out that it is not at all uncommon for epileptic children to be linked to phenomena and strange hallucinations.

The next incident that I remember happened when we were on holiday in Devon. There was a strange man, staying in the same bed and breakfast house as us, called Timothy, who was researching UFOs. He showed us pictures that he had taken of bright lights in the sky. I was too young to be interested in flying saucers but he had a lively dog called Blackie that was half collie.

One morning Blackie was missing so we went to look for him in the fields. After a while Lillian started crying and said she did not think he was alive. She was very upset and then had another of her epileptic seizures. She did not fall to the ground but was wobbling around, shaking her head and said she felt very dizzy. We managed to get her back to the holiday base and mum and dad put her to bed. We heard that Timothy eventually found his dog dead at the side of the road. Blackie had been hit by a car.

For a while after this Lillian was forced to take drugs to control her epilepsy but she hated taking them. She said they desensitised her so that she lost contact with her angels.

Today Lillian works as a therapist. She is one of these new-age holistic therapists who help people who are in an identity crisis. She seems to have outgrown her epilepsy problem and so no longer needs the Keppra drug to control her condition. She is very empathic and still has contact with her angels but says her most important work is done at night when she is asleep. She says she helps people who have just passed away move on towards the light because some souls are so shocked at dying that they are unable to move on. Lillian said that this is her life work and that she had been prepared for this role ever since she was a little girl.

Personally I have never had contact with angels, apart from witnessing the blue misty light in my room when I was very young, but Lillian has been guided by them for all her life. I do wonder if sensitive people are too readily drugged to stop them from having contact with these amazing celestial beings.

It was not the most romantic of proposals. One morning in May I woke up and thought that Carol and I might as well get married as a display of commitment to each other. I rolled over in bed and said, "Do you think we should get married?" Somewhat startled Carol replied, "Yes, why not?"

After breakfast we cycled through Richmond Park to the nearest registry office to find that you had to wait at least six weeks before you could book your wedding. We chose a Saturday at the end of my school term.

It was a wonderful day with just our close families present, with my spiritual teacher Antony being my best man and Carol's sister as her bridesmaid. We had morning tea at Pembroke Lodge in Richmond Park, then set off on the New Southern Belle for a boat trip down the Thames and spent several hours in the gardens at Hampton Court. It was the hottest day of the year but everyone was just bursting with happiness, especially me!

I think our families had given up all hope that Carol and I would ever conform enough to become formally married, so it was lovely to please everyone. However, Carol later disclosed that it had all been hard work for her, looking after her family and providing reception salads, sandwiches and whatnot for everybody, so maybe not the greatest day for her.[17]

In the early 1980s pregnant ladies did not usually have the option of knowing the sex of their foetus so for a bit of fun Carol would dowse for her clients and had a 100% record of guessing the right sex. Then one day her pendulum would not swing so Carol could not determine whether it was a boy or girl. This baby was still-born, which duly freaked her out so Carol did not dowse for her clients anymore, for she was unwilling to be cast in this sad situation again.

Then one day, circa 1985, it was Carol's turn to be surprised. She was busy treating one of her regular patients, who happened to be clairvoyant. This lady startled her by saying, "You do know you are pregnant, don't you?" After a tricky pregnancy our gifted, artistic daughter Kira was born early in the new year, making our little family unit complete.[18]

We had expected a healthy, robust child but Kira was always a challenge to Carol's homeopathic/ naturopathic philosophy, seemingly catching every possible cold germ in her vicinity and to boot disinclined to sleep at night. In homeopathic terms Kira was a 'tubercular type', probably through inheriting my mother's dodgy TB DNA. Battling with Kira's on-going health issues made it difficult for Carol to confidently treat her patients by just using homeopathic remedies, for if you are unable to fix your own child how can you expect to treat clients successfully?

Carol eventually shelved using homeopathy, as she had already ditched being an osteopath and acupuncturist. She retrained yet again using the 'spiritual' therapy techniques advocated by Brandon Bays with her 'journey' method and later Carol incorporated matrix energetics into her healing work.

As a toddler, Kira's favourite bedtime story was a book called, *The Bears' Bazaar*, which we probably read to her hundreds of times; Kira would always know when we deliberately missed a page of this book! In the story the bears made a variety of arty objects to sell at a church bazaar which seemed to inspire Kira to be creative for she was forever drawing or making things and today she is a creative force in the film industry.

One day Kira saw a fairy at the bottom of the garden.

She ran into the house as fast as she could. "Mummy, Mummy. There is a fairy in our garden!"

"Oh that's nice dear. Now be a good girl and finish your drink."

After she had finished her drink Kira went back into the garden and watched as the fairy gently fixed a butterfly's broken wing. The butterfly flew over the garden wall. Kira ran back into the house. "Mummy, Mummy. The fairy fixed the butterfly's broken wing and now it can fly again!"

"That's very kind of her. Now don't forget to tidy your room as nana will be here soon."

After she had tidied her room Kira went to look for the fairy. She found her in the rose bush uttering a spell to make the rose bush grow tall and strong. Kira ran back into the house. Nana Irene was sitting in a chair. "Nana, nana. We have a fairy in the garden and she is making the roses grow tall!"

"Oh how lovely," said Nana. "Now tell me how well you are doing at school?"

After she had gone to bed Kira had a dream about the fairy. The fairy said she was going to take her to see how rainbows were made. Kira woke up and got out of bed. She went down the stairs to the living room. Her father was watching football on the television. "Daddy, daddy. The fairy just spoke to me and said she was going to show me how rainbows are made!"

"Wow, that's fantastic!' said Daddy. "Now give me a big cuddle and go back to bed and don't forget to brush your teeth."

Next day it was raining but when the sun peeped out from behind a cloud Kira slipped out of the house and went into the garden. She found the fairy under the bird feeders. The fairy invoked a magic spell to make Kira tiny. Then they flew away over the roof-tops on the back of a beautiful white dove.

Not long after Kira was born I switched from Haringey to Surrey to work as a peripatetic remedial teacher. This job suited me very well as I drove around schools and taught small groups, or individual children how to read and write. These days the role would be called a Dyslexia teacher but in the mid-1980s Surrey was still in denial that dyslexia existed.

Teaching my young SEN children was a joy but the older pupils would often be more challenging, having experienced comparative failure for most of their school life. My colleague Jeanne was brilliant at dismantling their, 'I can't' attitude. She rather disdained using the familiar one-size-fits-all dyslexia teaching methods and treated every child as an individual. I followed suit by writing stories for my pupils, with them having starring roles in the stories, winning go-kart rallies, scoring goals, whatever their passion. I would sometimes take my guitar into school and have the pupils read/sing their own songs that we would write together.

More often than not I could teach my pupils to visualise their spellings and would encourage them to 'see' the letters big around the room in bright colours. Then I would get them to spell difficult words like 'millennium' forwards and backwards, which would completely bamboozle their class teacher and more importantly raise their self-esteem in front of their peers.

Occasionally Kira would join me for the day if she had an 'INSET' day at her school. I recall one afternoon struggling to draw a horse on the blackboard (it probably looked like a stick insect!) and Kira, at five years of age, stepped forward and drew an amazing little pony to the astonishment of my SEN group. They said, "She is a fantastic draw-er." Indeed she was and probably enjoyed putting one over her old man!

◈

Osho is an interesting case. He was named after the flamboyant Indian spiritual guru Osho Rajneesh, who encouraged his followers to follow principles of free love and to wear bright orange clothes in an otherwise austere Thatcherite London in the 1980s.

It is said that this Sannyasin love child was born with his eyes open inside an amniotic sac, a sure sign of an avatar. However, Osho was a difficult child in the sense that he did not sleep and was a finicky eater. He walked at nine months and suddenly started to speak whole words when barely one year old and was soon echoing his parents' conversations.

This little boy refused to attend nurseries, screaming for hours when separated from his mother. He avoided playing with other children and became fixated by domestic objects. Nothing was safe within his reach. He would take apart toasters, hair-dryers, anything really, and then reassemble them with his remarkable kinesthetic skills. Osho had this wonderful knack of repairing seemingly broken gadgets.

One day his father gave Osho his grandfather's watch, an old Seiko that had not worked for years. The watch became Osho's obsession. Two days later the watch was working well. After this Osho focused his attention on repairing time-pieces as his main form of play until a year or so later he became further distracted by computers.

It is said that Osho learnt to read simply so that he could peruse manuals to fix his beloved computers, for he was never much interested in reading stories of any kind. By the age of about four and a half Osho could repair most Microsoft computers.

School was a disaster from day one. He had no time for the other children, not even the school leavers who were asked to be his 'buddy' at break times. He effortlessly did the arithmetic exercises but had no interest in following phonic routines or learning grammar. He could already write sentences; his handwriting being a jerky print. He had no intention of writing made up stories and could see no point in drawing or painting. In fact he hated getting his hands dirty.

In PE lessons he would run wild, a lithe lean spirit that could do somersaults better than any other child but would not participate in any team games.

The educational psychologist labelled Osho autistic with high special needs so a Teaching Assistant was assigned to try to get Osho to comply with school discipline. These well-meaning ladies usually lasted about a term before being so frazzled they were replaced. Just sitting next to Osho would cause them palpitations so they would wonder if they had heart problems. But even worse, these kindly menopausal women would perspire like never before, often requiring a complete change of clothes at lunch time.

Eventually the class teachers would settle for the quiet life and allow Osho to 'play' with something like a broken Nintendo in the corner of the room and hope that an OFSTED inspection would not occur on their brief.

Then at the start of Year Three, an elderly ethnic Indian gentleman named Mr Manju took on the responsibility of being Osho's Teaching Assistant. He was a mystery man. No-one had ever seen him before and his address was baffling because it could not be located on a map but somehow his DSB (police disclosure) was confirmed in days rather than weeks.

Osho just beamed in Mr Manju's company and even began to participate in some of the school activities. He would now do the weekly spelling test, sometimes spelling the words backwards and upside down for fun and dictated sentences for his TA to write during the various class projects. In Games he would now take his turn during the skills sessions and follow procedures such as lifting balls over head or between legs in team games. He did all these activities with a bored glazed expression, leaving staff to wonder if Mr Manju had used a form of hypnosis to control him.

Using just a pencil and paper Osho finally began to draw during art lessons. At first the shapes were unspecific but over the weeks and months he began to draw in greater detail and they usually resembled exotic spacecraft, of the UFO kind. One day Osho drew a weird geometric design that looked a bit like a gateway. His class teacher complimented him. Osho said it was a star gate and that he was building an etheric star gate to fit over the school. Osho looked towards Mr Manju, who nodded and added mysteriously that this would help to raise consciousness.

One day the redoubtable Mrs Perkins cornered Mr Manju by the staffroom kitchenette as he made his elaborate Ceylon tea. She wanted to know how he had tamed Osho because she and several other TAs had been close to a nervous breakdown working alongside the wayward child. He answered that it was just a question of changing frequencies and when one hit on the right *vibration everything was fine. Mrs Perkins was somewhat bemused by this response!*

At the start of Year Four the school photographer gathered each class together to take both individual and group photos. For the first time Osho acquiesced in having his photograph taken with his class peers and can be duly seen in the glossy photo staring wanly at the camera, but there is no sign of his teaching assistant who everyone agreed had stood behind him.

I shall gloss over the dining hall difficulties because autistic children often refuse to eat with their peers and also the furore when Osho refused to participate in any of the annual school tests saying he had no need to prove himself.

The mystery of Osho culminated on the 21st December when he and his family simply vanished without trace and were never seen again. It was as if they suddenly walked out of their rented flat, leaving all their possessions behind and with the dining room lights left on. There was no goodbye note, no indication to family or friends that they might be moving away to another area and their battered Ford car was left in the parking lot.

To this day they are simply recorded on police records as 'missing'. Just another bleak statistic.

I had bought some tarot cards and decided to properly learn how to use them rather than self learn from a book. Following a recommendation I arranged to meet a tarot teacher, Terry the Tarot, in north London. I located his house and knocked on the front door, to be greeted by his French wife with a gallic, "Bonjour." She led me up the stairs to their work room. I shook hands with Terry, an affable Londoner and he indicated towards the 78 tarot cards, spread out on silk, like a mirror to all the possibilities for my soul. Breathtaking!

Terry was an excellent tutor and over the next few weeks I learnt the major and minor arcana with surprising ease, I think because this type of learning was an intuitive right-brained exercise. Having learnt the meaning of the singular cards you then focused on their position in the Celtic cross and how they could influence each other. The other students who were learning with Terry seemed to rely on channelling to help direct them but I simply read the cards.

Years later my healing tutor Ann told me that as a child she entered each card in her imagination, playing with the Fool's dog or wearing the crown of the High Priestess on her head, interlocking with them so that they became entwined with her own persona. She must have been an odd little girl!

After each tutorial Terry would ask me for a reading and he would listen intently as the images flew through my mind. But I did not see that in a few years he would be falsely accused of rape and later incarcerated for being a drug mule.[19]

When Kira was six years of age, I did a teacher exchange with an American SEN teacher. This was part of the famous Fulbright Classroom Teacher Exchange Program which offered educators the opportunity to exchange teaching positions with a teacher from another country. Our family duly spent a year in the regions of Chicago having exchanged houses as well as teaching roles.[20]

Kira flourished in her elementary school and Carol met many lovely people who were intrigued by her multi-therapist background. Carol was unable to practise in America as she did not have a Doctorate but shared her knowledge, such as first aid homeopathy, with her new-found friends, who returned the favour by whisking her off to see activities like ballet and plays in Chicago. From a social perspective it was an exciting year and we are still good friends with several families today.

I endured rather than enjoyed the teaching experience at my school, struggling somewhat to cope with the Illinois way of teaching Mathematics but enjoyed learning about American history and its constitution. It was a real bonus observing from within the US election in 1992, with Bill Clinton the democratic outsider beating the incumbent George Bush.

Perhaps the best part of the year was meeting up with both sides of our families in Florida. Carol's mother had never been abroad before and spent most of her time in wonder at being in Disneyland together with her grand-daughter who by now had acquired a broad Chicago accent!

Back in England my Literacy Support teaching role soon changed and I became an advisory teacher for the Surrey Learning and Language Support team. This meant that our teaching team were required to undergo a Language diploma course at Kingston University. I enjoyed the focus on linguistics and when the course finished spent a further year studying autism to gain more MA modules.

In 2001 I had a story published by Nelson Thornes called, *Grandmother's Secret*.[21] I had been a fan of the 'Spirals' series for reluctant adolescent readers and had frequently used the rather scary *Spirals* books to inspire my older pupils to read. I wrote several books in a similar vein for my Master's degree thesis but before I could submit any more stories for publication, Nelson Thornes were taken over by a German company and the fictional *Spirals* or *New Spirals* books were disbanded.

Grandmother's Secret was partially based on Dickens's concept in *A Christmas Carol* whereby Scrooge gets taken to the past, present and future. When my editor, Anita Jackson, deleted the 'past' section of the story. It felt a bit like having a limb cut off!

My grandfather had been in declining health for several years, struggling with his vision, hearing and rheumatoid arthritis:

It was just another November day with the wind stripping the last golden leaves from the trees. Inside the hospital the old engineer pulled himself up from his pillows. For the first time in weeks he was lucid and alert. He gave me a resigned look and repeated his given information.

"We had a meeting. I have to go into a home. Lily can't look after me anymore. She's not well. Her sisters will look after her. I have to go into a home."

The news had crushed him. He gazed into the space before him and pondered life without his Lily. The loss of living without his adored wife was just too much. He barely spoke again.

One week later a hearse carried my granddad Jack away from the dreaded care home.

Not long after this I received a phone call from Llandudno Hospital. My father Geoffrey was in a coma and they did not expect him to survive. They wanted my permission to turn off the life support machine. I said, 'No' but I would come at once. The least I could do was to make an effort to be at my father's side if he was about to leave our mortal coil.

I drove alone for four hours up the M1 and then along the M6 travelling through a fierce thunderstorm, with the rain beating down, unrelenting the whole way. The heavens seemed dismayed at the thought of my dad's imminent arrival.

Inside Llandudno Hospital I found his twisted form lying on a bed. His body lay littered with an array of wires sending messages to the life support machine. The lights flickered and beeped as he struggled to breathe through an oxygen mask.

For hour after hour I prayed for my stricken father, in particular asking for forgiveness for being such a lousy son. Then at about 2am Geoffrey stirred. He opened his contorted eyes and stared at me. He muttered something incomprehensible but he had somehow survived his ordeal and had come out of his coma. Staff came rushing in, gasped and said it was remarkable. They gently sedated him and he then slept peacefully so I crept away into the night.

In the morning I returned to be told that my father had suffered a terrible stroke. The Doctors mused that he had lain on the floor of his flat for several hours before someone responded to his faint cry for help. Later Geoffrey explained that it was as if someone had pushed him into a tiny cupboard, where he could hardly move or breathe. He spent months in hospital recuperating and had to learn to speak and walk again but he was always a gutsy man. I think he loved the challenge of proving everyone wrong. He said he fought for his life, "For my little Ricky!"

SIX

The Camden Oracle, Angels and Alchemy

ONCE A MONTH Carol would disappear for the day in North London to attend a gathering of healers, soothsayers and visionaries organised by her Matrix Energetics friend Candice. Geoff would manifest amongst them and the magic would begin.

If you met Geoff you might not see much beyond his tall engineer's gait and easy-going demeanour. Well into his eighties and suffering from reduced eyesight, he does not seek the limelight on our worldly terrain but on the ethereal plane he is a kind of witch-finder general, except for the fact that he resonates very well with the psychics, mediums and healers, who in a not-so-distant age would probably have been hanged for their special gifts to mankind.

Geoff works with his pendulum to remove a variety of entities, or an array of detrimental forces that can and do affect people's lives. He connects with healing energies that he surmises are available to him from his previous incarnations as a shaman. With these energies he can either disempower, destroy or redirect the detrimental energies from whence they came.

Sometimes the entities are not within his scope so he will then summon support from a spirit from a higher authority who will then deal with the issue. Geoff does not advertise his special kind of spiritual service; he simply makes himself available to his ever-growing band of friends by phone and people will usually find him by recommendation, or word of mouth.

Some of Geoff's cases are quite remarkable. For example he recently helped a woman in Scotland who kept having incidents whereby parts of her property would catch fire for no apparent reason. The police searched but could find no evidence of an arsonist, so in desperation she contacted Geoff who quickly linked the fires' origin back to the days of Lord Darnley, the husband of Mary Queen of Scots, who was murdered at Kirk O'Field when the house he was staying in burnt to the ground.

The woman's house, known as Port Mary House, was once part of Lord Darnley's estate. Back in the day a servant of Mary had used black magic to induce an entity to destroy the house because Darnley had attacked one of the servant's relatives. The servant wanted revenge! Although the house had been rebuilt in the eighteenth century the entity was still in residence at that location and was still trying to destroy the house as it had been originally instructed, hence the recurring fires.

Five hundred years after the initial fire, Geoff finally dealt with the ancient curse that had led to the original blaze and sent the entity back from whence it came. There have been no more reported fires on the property that had once been owned by Lord Darnley.

Anything can happen at Lena's Place.
You can sip green tea, maybe eat cake,
or try the Mediterranean cuisine.
But if you are feeling really brave,
come on the day when the psychics parade
at Lena's Place,

Coral will be there, with her angelic smile
and big, big hair.
She sits next to enigmatic Geoff,
up from Weston Supermare,
They will listen to your problems and fix them for you,
at Lena's Place.

To be sure Candy will be late.
But then she will entertain you with her news off the street;
threats against the homeless; pollution;
fracking; all kind of despicable acts.
Be assured Candy will fight for your rights
at Lena's Place.

Judith may have her crystals;
Candy her sparkling rings;
Coral plays with her tarot cards,
while Geoff twirls his dowsing string.
All this is happening when the psychics meet
at Lena's Place.

Henry may be fasting,
or ingesting magical things.
But while he contemplates which remedies to prescribe,
Geoff may dowse for him.
Together they will find a cure
at Lena's Place.

Carol will matrix your journey home,
to ensure you do not miss your train.
While Judith displays her meditation cards
That she channelled from etheric planes.
Meanwhile Mademoiselle Crystele recalls her shamanic rites
at Lena's Place.

Simon explains the karma behind
an insidious voodoo spell.
As he battles against injustice
and fights to regain his health.
This seer sits like a Buddha supreme
at Lena's Place.

Moira pores over her astrology books,
taking notes of time of birth.

While Ria regales with her conspiracy tales;
how the illuminati control all power on Earth.
while Julia sits like an Egyptian Queen
at Lena's place.

So if you have a mystery to solve,
or need an evil spell to break,
or want to discuss alien miens,
or discover why people go missing without trace.
Then go meet the psychics and seers
at Lena's Place.

Bastia the oracle can see things that really ought to be beyond the human eye. Some of us can sense an entity from another dimension when in a darkened atmosphere, or get a glimpse of a spirit from the corner of our eye but Bastia is blessed with her holy clairvoyance, a blessing that can also be a curse. She revealed her vision of the Birdman to her mystic brethren as they gathered at Lena's place.

At dusk we are familiar with the sight of swarming birds as they swoop together preparing for their nightly roosting, hiding safely away from human gaze. In their hundreds, nay thousands, they gather and once together manifest as one great soul force with their angelic creator at the centre of their being. How beautiful it must have been all those years ago to create these beautiful birds, a vision of angelic thought and love!

But the human planet guardians are behaving ever more irresponsibly, with their poisonous pesticides, increasing air pollution and ever more violent actions against each other that cause such concern to all the elemental kingdoms. How the birds suffer in their domain as their natural breeding grounds are cemented over, time and again, by yet another block of ghastly apartments.

So one day the suffering Birdman embodied like Throth on a park bench, accompanied by hundreds of birds who tried to hide him with their wings. His tiny figure, sitting dressed in black, held up cones of bird seed to feed his flock. It is unclear if the Bird-man had been forced down from the heavens into permanent human form or had simply assumed the guise of a Filipino gentleman whilst he manifested himself to Bastia.

The beauty of this angelic being was immediately apparent to Bastia who watched in wonder as the birds fluttered all over him like an ongoing caress. But then she felt his pain and knew that she had to absorb the suffering, to free and re-energise his angelic form so that he could soar with renewed hope that not all humans were antagonistic to nature and birds in particular.

That night Bastia conversed with her shaman friend from the west country and together they transformed the Birdman's vibration by divining light and love into his vital frequency.

She saw him again a few days later, this time far more energised and wearing lighter clothes. Her friend secretly took his photograph, a vision of wings and beauty, but when she tried to follow him back to his lodgings he easily eluded her and was never seen in the park again.

Last summer they called me the bird man
When I found you beneath a tree.
A mass of beak and feathers,
You made a nest right out of me.

I fed you with my fingers.
Together we searched for worms,
Digging earth at four in the morning.
At the time you were my curse.

I remember you my drunken bird
Sipping wine from my mother's glass;
Flapping across the garden,
Crashing into the grass.

The day came when I had to let you go,
It was time to set you free.
I watched as you turned in the sky
And then you flew right back to me.

You are mine and you'll always be mine,
No matter what they do or say.
Inside we are linked together,
In some weird and mysterious way.

Bastia would often engage us by describing her interaction with the elementals. One of her favourite adventures featured a fox that she would occasionally feed. It lived in a nearby copse. One evening, led by her compassion, Bastia followed the fox into the wood with food in her hand to feed her favourite waif. To her astonishment she watched as the fox metamorphosed into a handsome young man. In her vision he seemed to be sleeping, naked on the ground, but then turned to look at her as she slowly backed out of the copse.

The fox trailed after her as she drifted home and she felt almost at one with this beautiful creature as she fed him by hand through the railings.

Most people regard foxes as creatures of low cunning but to Bastia her fox represented a subtle spirit of sublime beauty. A gifted artist, she painted her fox with a mortal knowing, its tail swishing with a demonstrative flourish as if to say, 'I am here to represent nature with all its natural intelligence.'

In Glastonbury, darkness descended upon the church wall. Inside the church, the congregation slowly entered and took their place within the wooden pews. They sang their hymns and listened intently to the biblical stories offering hope to all mankind.

Can heaven be built upon the earth? The church-goers sipped their juice and ate their wafer bread that represented the substance of Christ their saviour. Homeward they slipped past the frozen wall, unaware of the atrocities that have been committed over the ages by the side of their church.

Nearby, but on another frequency, passing souls were enticed away from following their final destiny to the light by a dark lord, who captivated his victims by whispering to them their own secret desires. Seduced by his lewd promises, they followed the dark lord as he drew them down, down and further down until they were swollen by their own sensuous appetite and became trapped in a lower entity. And then he imprisoned these unfortunate earthbound souls by transplanting their helpless forms inside the silent church wall, where they lay like little lost gargoyles way beyond the gaze of the passing public eye.

But Demeter has tired of such evil behaviour and sent her oracle to save these poor lost souls. She opened Bastia's eyes by casting a seeing spell upon the light of a new day.

Bastia opened the window of her friend's home and gazed towards the lovely church but all she could see were the agonised faces of the trapped souls as they lay concealed inside the church wall. She could see their mouths wailing but no-one could hear their despairing cries for help. They were suffering and she could see how their souls were disintegrating into a lower form and knew that she had been chosen to release these poor souls from their terrible fate.

Instinctively Bastia knew to photograph the terror that she could see in the wall, for Bastia's innate compassion would send light to release the nefarious entrapment. With one click of the flashing camera the dark lord's evil spell was broken and the poor souls escaped to find their way back to the light within. The wall was now laid bare of its victims, just an ordinary church wall.

But the joy of this release was short-lived for now Bastia's own anguish began. Tears began to trickle down her face as she relived the terrible sorrow that she had witnessed as she absorbed their agonising pain. Then she found that she was buffeted from all sides as people turned against her in all kinds of spiteful ways. It was as if the dark lord was vengeful and sought any way to drag her down.

For days and weeks Bastia cried and cried until time passed on by and the suffering she had seen became less prominent in her mind and her friends gradually became kindly to her again.

When our lovely Persian cat Angel died, a few months shy of twenty years of age, we asked the oracle if she had any information from the other side? Bastia went into a meditative state for a few minutes and then told us that Angel now resided on Syrius 'B' as a beautiful woman. There was no message, for Angel knew that she had accomplished her mission of bringing love and joy into our lives.

Whilst comforted by the thought of Angel's metamorphosis into human form, albeit on a different star system, it did make me wonder if on Syrius 'B' roles were reversed and I would eventually find myself deployed as Angel's pet rabbit, cat or mouse!

When Archimedes came to live in Camden he turned heads with his easy-going manner and cool looks. He was an accomplished musician and would meditate for hours, sitting cross-legged on a rug in front of his girlfriend's electric fire. He would not reveal much about his past, just that he had spent many years practising shamanic healing at the Inner Sanctuary, somewhere in Mexico.

Archimedes had a hypnotic quality about him; people opened up to him and would pour out their worries and often solve their own issues without him saying a word. He was renowned for finding lost objects by dowsing with his crystal pendulum but he was not keen to foretell futures, saying he should not interfere with people's karma. This did not prevent him from occasionally making money using binary mathematical algorithms on the stock market.

Unfortunately his beautiful spiritual manner had a shadow side that would erupt particularly if he had taken a chemical substance, or over-indulged in alcohol. Then he would scream at his attractive partner and beat her with his fists. It was as if dark maladies took possession of his body, for the following day Archimedes would be in complete denial that he had lost control of his mind.

After a particularly savage beating Bastia entered the fray to protect her neighbour and friend. She insisted that Archimedes leave the building and they stood face to face shrieking and snarling at each other, like a coyote attacking a rabid fox. Someone had to stand down and eventually the coyote backed away, slowly cursing the gifted clairvoyant as he left the room, never to return.

Deep into the night Bastia was awakened from her slumber by creaking floorboards. Something was entering the room from under the bed! The wood seemed to splinter as a massive rat hauled itself into the bedroom and attacked Bastia, running up her legs and arms and sinking its teeth into her shoulder. This etheric rat did not belong to this physical world and vanished at the sound of Bastia's screams, its mission now complete.

So the price that Bastia paid for evicting the shaman from her friend's apartment was a year of broken sleep, for she was afraid that the metaphysical rat would return and attack her again. It was only when her inner guides led her to acquire her magical cat Merlin that she could once again rest in peace at night, guarded by her feline friend.

Pythia has arisen from her slumbers
but alas she no longer resides on the slopes of Mount Parnassus,
where the sun once set upon her holy mount,
as she transmitted her startling prophecies,
uttering strange dactylic hexameters,
delivering salutary messages from the gods.

For now the Delphic oracle
has decamped into the 21st century,
living alone in the busy suburb of Camden.
Once again she listens to her muses,
channelling the sun god Apollo;
aiding suffering souls in her sublime holy temple.

When Simon attempted to remove some mould from his mother's house he had little idea that he was opening a Pandora's box that would absolutely ruin his life. A gifted technician, Simon was confident that the chemical he had chosen would remove the substance but fate intervened and instead he became infected by the toxic mould that kept on recurring, affecting his personal health, no matter how often he purified his diet or changed his clothes.

Everywhere you look there are micro toxins in the air. Some are natural, like the fungi you see growing on trees but many are created by man's folly, such as using lead paint or by creating humid environments within houses where moulds can grow and mutate. For a spiritual person like Simon it begs the question, why should he be brought down so low by these toxic chemicals? He speaks darkly of a voodoo curse that he is unable to break. But I wonder if he is having to repay the consequences of a previous life, when he had full control over chemical substances but misapplied his arcane skills for financial gain.

Christos was an unusual priest. To his parishioners he conducted himself with considerable grace being fully devoted to the Mass and Eucharist rituals. He observed the divine liturgy tradition, by reading from the scriptures, partaking of wine and bread to represent the blood and body of Jesus Christ the saviour and ensured that there was always a collection for the poor of his parish.

He followed the Greek Orthodox tradition of abstinence from worldly pleasures that for him culminated in a ten-day fast during the winter Lent. Christos would only partake of water in his system as he sought for a divine presence within. For Christos had a questioning mind and sought far and wide for the immortality of his soul. He wanted to know the divine secrets, not to blindly believe like his parishioners. In the heat of the day he would hallucinate and see visions in the shadows of his church. It was during one of these extended fasts that he began to hear a voice purporting to be St Barnabas and in time this voice became his inner guide.

There was one man within his parish who both intrigued and troubled him. He was an elderly man named Alim of Arab descent. He was rumoured to be over ninety years of age but he still traded in wine and fine foods and was rarely ill. Whenever they met he was always courteous to Christos but understandably never entered his church. Christos assumed that Alim was a non-practising Muslim but at Easter and after Lent Alim always generously donated a large box of food for the poor people of the parish. After one such occasion, prompted by his inner voice, Christos decided to visit Alim to thank him personally for his food parcels.

Christos walked slowly up the slope to the north side of the town as he was suffering from shingles following his latest fast. He approached the Arab's house and knocked on the front door but there was no reply. Christos found the old man tending to the herbs in his garden. Alim looked up and welcomed the priest with a smile and a gesture to enter the house through the back door.

They sat at a table and Alim offered the priest mint tea. Christos accepted and duly thanked Alim for his gifts. He was genuinely impressed by the old man's sprightly demeanour and questioned him about his trading.

Alim explained that his son had run the wine business but this had recently been curtailed. He himself passed the time exploring the transformation of both metals and minerals, for he was an alchemist and practised transmuting detrimental energies, amongst other things finding natural cures for common illnesses.

He had noticed Christos wincing in pain and offered him an elixir to alleviate the shingles pain but the priest declined, preferring to endure his suffering. Alim surprised Christos by saying that his time on Earth was fast running out. He had seen the beautiful angel of death in the corner of his study so that he knew that his life was approaching the end. He looked the priest in the eye, took a deep breath and attempted to unburden himself by revealing the following story.

I called you to me. I used my alchemy. That is why you chose to visit me today and are sitting here in my kitchen. I thank you for coming. I probably only have hours left to live on our beautiful planet and I need to finalise arrangements about my property but more than that I need to exorcise a demon that has latched onto my soul.

My son is a clever businessman but his morals are weak. Many years ago he killed a prostitute when high on drugs. In his delirium he thought she was a snake, so he strangled her. Then he panicked and brought her body to me. He probably thought I could bring her back to life but she was long dead. I should have done the right thing and called the police but I am human and I love my son, despite all his frailties so I agreed to get rid of the body. For me this is an easy process of dissolving the body with Aqua Regia, which is a form of sulphuric acid.

I thought that would draw the curtain down on this despicable act but I was wrong. The prostitute belonged to the Russian mafia and they hunted down my son.

Tortured, he told them how I had got rid of the body and so they spared his life but targeted me. They threatened me, a religious man like yourself, unless I co-operated with them to remove the evidence of their victims. So my home became a crematorium of the missing. Once in a while they would fetch a body to me, always in the middle of the night and I would set about dissolving the flesh and bones. The Aqua Regia would leave no trace, even dissolving the teeth of the poor victims. Each time I wept and said prayers for the dead but I knew I was in the thrall of evil and feared for my soul. I am frightened for my karma because unlike you I know I will have to pay back the crimes of this life in another human incarnation and I fear that I will be disfigured, or worse.

My son has now left the island never to return. He has a new identity and may be safe for the rest of his life, unless he reactivates his foolish sensuous ways. Who knows, that is his choice but the Russians are ruthless and will track him down if he leaves them any opportunity.

As an act of atonement for my considerable sins, I will leave my property and land here on Cyprus to the orphans and poor widows. These papers are signed and I leave them with you, the most honest man I have heard of in this region, to finalise with the appropriate authorities.

I thank you and ask for your Christian prayers for the poor unknown victims. For myself I pray that Allah is indeed merciful and forgiving: 'Rabbi inni zalamto nafsi faghfirli.'

Soon after this, Christos left the building leaving Alim kneeling on the floor uttering his Islamic prayers. Christos *carried a parchment of papers under his arm. He would deal with them tomorrow. Both tired and astonished by what he had heard, he headed towards his church compelled by his compassion to pray for the suffering of the victims. He knew that he was duly responsible to inform the police but that too could wait until tomorrow. As he walked back down the hill he noticed that the wind had picked up. By the time he reached the sanctuary of his church the wind had transformed into a gale. He had to wrap both hands around his papers to avoid them being swept away.*

All night the storm howled, tearing tiles off houses and ripping branches from vulnerable trees. It was the worst storm to affect Cyprus in years but had only affected the small region of Christos's village.

In the morning Christos stepped through the carnage of the storm to first visit the police and then later passed Alim's papers to the local solicitor. Shortly after his return home he received news that Alim had been found dead but fully clothed on his bed. Christos again entered his church to light another candle for the alchemist and prayed that he would be forgiven by his creator.

At Lena's Place, Henry sat at the end of the table like a holy potentiate amongst the soothsayers and healers. Whilst we contemplated earthly concerns such as invasion of privacy, health issues and abominable acts of astral violence he focused on delivering our planet from unmitigated disaster. Henry, in his appointed role as a universal grail practitioner, concentrated his energies on transforming our planet's upper universe. This meant raising the consciousness of like-minded souls to duly purify the magnetic currents in our upper atmosphere. We listen intently as Henry patiently engages with us to share his spiritual solutions and we wonder when our planet's ascension will truly begin.

SEVEN

Healing Amongst the Shamans

FOR THE LAST thirteen years of my teaching career I worked for Surrey's prestigious Physical and Sensory Support, which had three teams for hearing impairment, visual impairment and physical disability. Surrey did not have a school for physical disability and had an inclusion policy whereby all children should be taught in mainstream schools, whenever possible. There were a few schools with PD units attached but in time these were gradually filled with autistic children who were difficult to teach.

Over the years I had noticed more and more autistic children in mainstream school classes and this does beg the question, why? As someone who has never been vaccinated, despite all manner of threats and scares as a child, I think babies are over-vaccinated, weakening their natural immunity system. If you fiddle with nature there will most likely be a price to pay but of course there are many other factors that may lead to autism, including lead in the air, fast food intake and so on.

My job was very variable. In theory I could be in a Nursery or Reception class advising about the education, or setting, of the disabled child in the morning and then in the afternoon be sitting alongside a student in a college, tutoring them to attain their A level in a subject such as Philosophy or Psychology. I loved this variation in my advisory teaching role and would step in and out of my personas with ease: uncle Richard with the tots and very professional Mr Kemble with the older students!

At work David and I would sometimes have interesting discussions about our religious beliefs. David held traditional Christian values and justified his belief in Jesus as the Son of God by the importance of his death and resurrection, saying that Jesus died for the sins of mankind. He believed in the Bible as the word of God and that the stories were mainly factual, not analogies as I would try to argue. He would listen non-plussed as I stated that Jesus, being a Nazarine would have been a vegetarian and would never have offered fishes as food to his followers.

One cold winter's day Carol and I visited David and his family at their church in Cranleigh. It was a bright newly-built church, which many of the parishioners had helped to build, either physically or by fundraising.

We were impressed by the vital atmosphere, for you had the feeling that individual souls became at one and thus strengthened when united with the whole congregation. There were probably more than sixty people present and that was after the children had been hived off to their Sunday School. Whatever the religious beliefs, socially this Baptist church was a rousing success. I thought to myself how lovely it would be to belong to a community of souls like this. For they were compassionate people who really seemed to care for the elderly and sick and who gave such a wonderful farewell to a pastor who was moving to a different county.

But listening to the Bible readings, (including John 21) I realised I could never accept the Bible stories at face value because they all seemed designed to create hero worship of Jesus: 'Believe in Jesus and you will be saved!' I knew that no-one in this church would be interested in the mystic interpretation of this little saga; with the fish representing mysteries, the numbers most relevant and with the boat representing the soul, with the command to listen to one's (right sided) intuition.

We had experienced similar feelings in Kentucky with our delightful Christian friends Jim and Jennie, the difference being that their church was like a whole village! Carol and I have so much respect for people like David and Jim who always attempt to walk their talk and make you feel welcome, putting aside any personal religious beliefs.

One of the benefits of my peripatetic advisory teacher role was being able to explore the beautiful south-west Surrey terrain, from Haslemere to Guildford and Cranleigh to Farnham.

At weekends Carol and I would visit some of the pretty locations.

A particular favourite of mine was Shere and we would sometimes end up meditating at the Harry Edwards Healing Sanctuary, on 'Harry's Cherry Tree Walk'. On one occasion whilst in a deep meditative state I heard a tiny sound to my left-hand side. I opened my eyes to see a weasel walking within a metre of me. I nudged Carol and we watched as the weasel, who was totally unaware of our presence, walked slowly past us, absorbed by the rabbits he could see in the pasture about a hundred yards away. It was quite a treat to see such a handsome wild animal, with his bright orange coat and white underbelly. Later the thought came to me that the weasel could be my spirit animal but I hoped not! An eagle or stag, oh yes! but not a weasel or rat.

Not long after this, I decided to honour my dad, who had died in 2009, by undergoing a healing course at the aforementioned Harry Edwards Healing Sanctuary.[22]

Harry Edwards had actually healed my mother of TB back in the 1940s when she was eighteen years of age.

We had three excellent tutors: Carol, who would regale us with her shaman stories; lovely, calm Ann, who always seemed to operate from her heart centre and Sheila who would have been a perfect fit at Harry Potter's 'Hogwarts School,' with her fulsome knowledge of crystals and elixirs.

One of the onerous aspects of the course was to do a hundred healings, most of them away from the sanctuary. One day I was doing a chair healing on my mother and had finished doing the circuit around the body. I stood up from her feet and walked around her chair to complete the healing at her shoulders as we had been taught. I was astonished to have the feeling that someone else was giving her healing!

I had the strong impression that a male figure, quite a large man, wearing a light blue shirt and light-coloured slacks, was working on my mother's shoulders. So I had the momentary bizarre decision to make, whether to step back and watch this figure or to move forward to finish my healing session. I decided on the latter, so I moved through this other figure to complete my healing. But as I moved forward to place my hands on my mother's shoulders I felt as if I moved through layers of liquid, like a filmy substance.

So who was this figure? It was not my father, who was shorter than me and not my step-dad, who was six feet four inches tall. The figure looked a little bit like my spiritual teacher Antony Bates but he was not a healer as it was not his role. If this male figure had worn a white coat I might have thought it was Harry Edwards but this would be unlikely as this healing was not taking place at the healing sanctuary.

Who is this ageing oaf trying to kid?
What is he doing wafting his hands
around, as if he could heal anyone?
Can people not see what a fraud he is?
He cannot heal himself let alone anyone else.

He says he has wrapped himself in the clothes of a redeemer
and has cast off his old foolish ways.
Does he really think that because he has read a few books
that he has anything useful to say?

At the Harry Edwards healing sanctuary it was not encouraged to promote spiritualism, even though the great man had once been the president of the NFSH, but as students we would hear about extraordinary incidents and discuss them amongst ourselves.

When it first happened Doris said she was totally
dumbfounded. Her long-retired husband Bob had sat
down in the lounge after an afternoon's toil in the garden
and proceeded to take his afternoon nap. However, instead

of his usual gentle snores Bob started uttering sentences in a strange mechanical voice. At first Doris did not know what to do but after a while she realised her husband was channelling something and started to take notes using her old secretarial shorthand skills which she had not used for more than twelve years.

The walk-in voice did not say who it was but simply said it was offering advice for mankind and that Bob and Doris had been the chosen vehicles because they were good people and had been regular attendees at the local spiritualist church.

The voice, obviously male, was at least two octaves lower than Bob's and had an unusual accent, perhaps Egyptian. Doris was used to the clairaudient leader at her local spooks' church, as she called it, but she had never participated in a trance session before. It was quite riveting for her Bob to be chosen as a messenger. After she had recovered from her initial shock she beamed with pride that Bob was giving forth such important information about the afterlife.

The voice said that people needed to know that on the other side there was no sudden divergence into heaven and hell. People passed over with their natural vibration and their own way of being and they would go to the place that was most appropriate to them. So if they had led a wicked life they would go to a sphere with like-minded souls on the lower astral plane. The majority of souls who had led nondescript lives, neither saints nor sinners, would go to a higher sphere and would review their life with their given guide but no judgements would be made by any higher beings. There was no fiery judgemental God. Souls would see for themselves the opportunities they had missed or the bad decisions they had made and make their own judgments and would no doubt pay the consequence for their past actions with their future karma.

Doris was reassured that life beyond the physical plane was far more satisfactory than on Earth. Souls would choose their environment, rather like creating a virtual home, which could be a beautiful sea-shore location, a river or a mountain view. They would stay there with their family and friends until they decided they were ready to move on, to make progress with their ultimate goal of being at one with the divine, an embodiment of love.

Some souls would crave to return to Earth, which had a much denser vibration. They missed the lure of sex, drugs and rock and roll and the pleasures of materialism. Some souls would volunteer to return to the 'wild west' of our planet in the role of a spiritual teacher but it was very easy to become lost in the materialistic void and to lose your spiritual vocation.

The voice emphasised how souls should always aspire upwards, to manifest light and love but ultimately it was the individual soul's decision because we all had free will and nobody forced us to do anything, although higher souls were always available for counsel and to advise.

When the Egyptian voice departed, Bob finally opened his eyes. He knew that he had been used as a channel, indeed inwardly he had given his permission but he had no concept of what had been transmitted through him. He was now very tired and savoured his cup of tea as

Doris fussed around him and read back what had been uttered.

Tina is one of the healers at the centre. When she describes her Giant entities to me I have to remember that as a shaman she operates from a transcended state of consciousness, so her answers to my mindful questions are more about feelings rather than anything rational.

For example, I am curious about the role of her Giants, or Titans, during the creation of the world and how they cope now as mankind continues to wage war on different races and generally endanger nature. But Tina just marvels about their vastness and chuckles at their disdain of human actions. She has recently been to Wales to explore a valley of the Giants and met an indignant 'little Giant' who encouraged her to urinate on a barbed wire fence to help rust it away as he was against anything that prevented trespass onto a field.

Tina's shamanic vision is all about this type of freedom of movement in nature. She aspires to live in the here and now, to give and take, including to eat what you like, justifying her food philosophy by pointing at a blackbird digging up a worm, who in turn may soon be the prey of a cat.

She is wired again, this shamanic healer,
with her hyena laugh and flame red hair.
For she senses their presence, her mysterious kin
from the outermost spheres.
She calls to them and they will reply,
for she is the keeper of the elves.

She understands well these chameleon spirits
who spend their time transmuting light from stone.
For gems and jewels are little lost fragments of souls
whose love became trapped in materialised gold.
They trust her, shamanic Tina,
Earth mother of the elves.

Usually they appear when they are weary,
worn or disgruntled at the end of a weather beaten day.
Or when they flee from the dark Lord
who seeks them as his prey.
Then they seek sanctuary in the care of Tina,
Shamanic healer of the elves.

But these are not easy guests to receive
for they meddle with gravity
and play in their mischievous way;
malfunctioning electricity,
Moving objects around, especially her jewellery.
Viva! Tina, patient protector of the elves!

She meditated and fasted for twenty-four hours before heading off to her shamanic gathering. They met in a remote field, close to a sacred space that had been dutifully prepared days beforehand. United together they drummed and chanted around the great fire that burned and roared as a token of their earthly sins and suffering.

They set about their rituals, smudging their bodies with sage charcoal and paced around the fire that was positioned precisely to the East of the sweat lodge. The chanting became more intense as they tossed sage in the four directions and uttered "rrrr" to the East, "ehhh to the south and "eeee"and "ohhhh" to the West and North, finally sounding "ooouuu" to the centre of the cauldron.

Each shaman placed a much-loved relic on the altar situated outside the tepee and then one by one they passed the sweat lodge door keeper, who uttered his strange words of welcome and smudged them once again with sage as they entered his smokey domain. They crawled clockwise until they found their favoured position in front of the sizzling stones and began to chant or sing together to connect with the Great Spirit above, or ancestors from the underworld. Some would confront their demons, others would have miraculous healing and a few would unite with nature spirits and ride unicorns, or rise up into an angelic world.

There were four rounds to endure, with water provided outside the lodge. Some would choose to be naked, others would drift away on their own personal psychotropic journey but all would try to endure each of the four rounds of systematic chanting and singing despite sweating from every pore, with the intense heat from the stones seemingly sapping all the oxygen from the air, finally leaving the sweat lodge quivering in an altered state, barely able to move.

Each experience would be different. No-one could anticipate what might happen. But everyone enjoyed the aftermath, a frolic in water and with cooked food to break the fast.

My mother frowned as she listened to the shaman's description of the sweat lodge, for she did not believe in trying to force things to happen. I persuaded mum to describe her own mystic experience in Plymouth, whereby she glimpsed a tiny bright light far away in the night sky and watched fascinated as this light travelled at tremendous speed towards her, growing bigger and bigger until it dramatically multiplied into three large balls, each coloured orange and red, that glistened in the sky above her as she stood at her upper floor window.

Mum said she looked down into the street below but to her amazement no-one walking or driving appeared to notice these dazzling apparitions and to her dismay she could not persuade her sleeping husband to awaken. The balls hovered in the sky for quite a while but then suddenly shimmered as they rejoined as one and then hurtled back from whence they had come, to leave my mother breathless, in amazement at what she had seen, for she realised it had been an inner vision and she wondered if it was a portent or a message from the beyond.

We had heard about a psychic surgeon, who was based at Chelmsford and made the effort to visit his clinic. [23] His waiting room was a wondrous shrine to Sai Baba, the rather exotic Indian guru. After paying our twenty pounds we sat amongst the Indian meditators and gazed at the flowers and messages of love and thanks that were placed on the shrine.

After a considerable wait and many, many blessings, my mother was finally called into the treatment room. She sat in a chair and gazed up at Stephen Turoff, who at six feet five inches is a healer from the east end of London. She explained that she was blind in her right eye and would appreciate some healing. Stephen regaled her with his cockney patter and placed his large hands around her eye. We watched amid the silence and hoped for a miracle. After her healing Stephen appeared to pluck some vibhuti (holy ash) from the air and gave mum a mark on her forehead, which is meant to protect her from evil forces.

It was Carol's turn next. She asked for healing on her troublesome right side that might be related to her gallbladder, or liver. Carol enquired whether Stephen was a vegetarian because she likes her practitioners to aspire to a pure body and mind. Stephen scoffed at this notion and took the broad line that, "God is not a vegetarian. God is everything."

He then set about performing a psychic operation on Carol. What I witnessed does not in any way make any sense to my mind. I saw Stephen take a blunt instrument, scissors I think and opened up Carol's midriff. He then placed his hand inside Carol's stomach and one by one, removed some dark substances which he nonchalantly tossed into the waste paper basket. You could hear the substances go, 'plop!', as they landed in the bin. Then he appeared to press together the layers of skin to seal the wound on Carol's stomach. This psychic operation lasted for perhaps ten minutes. Carol said that when she glimpsed into the waste bin, there was nothing there!

Then it was my turn. I lay on the treatment table in some trepidation. I told Stephen that as far as I knew I did not have anything wrong with me but Stephen assured me that I required some work on my bowels. I closed my eyes and Stephen busied himself with my lower midriff area with Carol observing from her chair about five metres away. I also heard the same 'plop! sound as waste material from my body was bunged into the bin. Finally I opened my eyes to find Stephen gazing at me with his hand on my forehead. He said some beautiful words about angels and flowers and I felt genuine love for him, which surprised me because

I am usually very defensive about opening up to any kind of man love.

Afterwards, somewhat dazed, Carol and I checked our stomachs for signs of blood and gore and were rather amazed to see what appeared to be four-inch scars scourged across our bodies. These scars slowly disappeared after about four days.

I asked my mum if she could see better out of her right eye. "No," she replied. "In fact I can't see anything at all with all this bloody ash in my eye!"

I was not very good at keeping in contact with my old friends and colleagues but I would occasionally meet the shaman, who for the purposes of this story I will call Raven, at Green fairs (and Carol once enrolled him into one of her esoteric evening classes). There were always legendary stories about this remarkable man.

It was a such a shock to her, to have cancer. All the medical advice said to go down the chemo route but her best friend had died shortly after receiving chemotherapy. Her body had turned a septic orange colour, like a damaged fruit. She knew it was not for her. She decided to go on a fruitarian diet and considered going to the Hippocrates Institute in Florida but then she heard about this strange young healer, with long matted hair, who worked in a West London practice. He was a wizard of sorts and could do magic with his crystals and runes. His shamanic name was Raven and she arranged to meet him the following day.

With trepidation she stepped inside his dark lounge and gazed around at the beautiful natural rocks, gems and exotic coprolites that were so mesmerising with their dull natural light. There were crystals of all shapes and colours everywhere, but where was this exotic young man, this sorcerer, this healer of body and mind?

He was standing right in front of her; invisible to her eye. She was startled when she finally saw him. He gazed at her for a while and then said in his gentle voice, "You have cancer. I can smell it." He looked at her acutely. "He pointed to her left breast and then to her lymph gland area. "It is here, and there."

He said he would help her. She would not die, for it was not her turn to leave these outer planes. He would help her to get rid of the cancer. She did not have to pay him for a year and then she would pay him what she felt he deserved. Shaken and strangely relieved, she agreed.

Raven left her with his assistant whilst he rummaged at the back of his room searching for the appropriate crystal. Then he summoned her to a table and she sat down while he lit incense and cast his runes. The runes indicated that she had to have this psychic operation next week under a full moon. He explained that she had to leave her body for a while whilst he dealt with the cancer. He would take her onto a different frequency using Amanita Muscaria. She would probably sleep and have vivid dreams. She agreed to see him again next Tuesday at her own apartment.

Time seemed to crawl by but at last it was Tuesday and dusk was drawing in after a dull uneventful day. Then Raven arrived with his female assistant carrying two large bags. He laid a colourful blanket upon the floor and cast his runes. They were positive so he moved around the room placing crystals in a shape like a star. He carefully measured out the grams of Fly Agaric into a bowl and poured boiling water over the mixture, stirring all the time and muttering a mantra that she could not understand. He added sugar and something else, it may have been tea, to the mixture. Her head was already dizzy with the strong incense smell burning in the room.

She sat and meditated in the centre of the star design and started to sip the cooling elixir. It tasted dreadful but almost at once she relaxed into an altered state of consciousness, so she kept sipping the drink and gradually became at one with the universe as her pulse emanated an energy that made her feel invincible. She felt as if a divine being was bursting through her muscles, making her feel like Superwoman. Time had no meaning at all, as seconds seemed to last for eons. And then she seemed to be sucked away into another cosmos and saw herself lying on a table being examined by the gods and there at the heart of them was Raven her healer. He theatrically displayed a beautiful crystal and then held it over her left side as the divine beings chanted in unison. The voices were beautiful, pitching higher and higher until the sound suddenly stopped and she started to fall, tumbling like Alice down her rabbit hole and then she soundly slept.

The next day she had this vile taste in her mouth but felt buoyant! She just knew that she was okay but was desperate to see the shaman. She drove to the healer's practice and sat in the tiny waiting room. She could hear Raven on the phone speaking to a client. When he had finished his call his assistant ushered her into his exotic lounge and he lifted a box onto the table. Inside the box she recognised the beautiful rose quartz crystal that Raven had selected for her healing, but now it was black! He explained that the crystal now contained the cancer that had been in her body and that she was cancer free!

We like to think that we have free will but sometimes things happen that seem preordained. Mike told me about his uncle who, with some friends, played around with an Ouija board. After a while they were invited to ask the 'spirit', who was communicating via the Ouija board, some questions. Mike's uncle, very much part of the racing fraternity, asked for the winner of the 'Derby.' The Ouija board duly tapped out the horse's name. When no-one else asked a question, Mike's uncle asked for the winner of the 'Oaks'.

Somewhat trustingly, Mike's uncle placed a lot of money on these spirit tips as a double, and won enough money to buy a house. It could be argued that the spirit was simply a good tipster but what if the race had already been decided? If something as insignificant as a horse race can be already determined then what about all the important issues in life, such as wars, life and death?[24]

After treating the initial rush of clients at the healing clinic we had some spare time to decorate the treatment room with little eucalyptus branches hewn from the garden; for this beautiful tree has excellent healing properties as well as a sublime aroma. Before we had completed laying out the eucalyptus we had a surprise drop-in client, a well-known artist who specialised in doing spirit drawings.

When Linda accompanied this artist into the treatment room I was surprised to feel the air chill despite it being a warm summer's day. I closed the window and sat on a chair and listened as this lady introduced herself.

She said her name was Maria. By appearance she looked like an ancient Goth with her dark, almost black eyes and pale translucent skin, her rather plain face topped by an extraordinary fuzz of thick-set red hair. She was dressed from head to toe in plain navy-blue but her thin hands were decorated by three magnificent rings; later she told us they were a sparkling sapphire, a deep-set ruby and an enormous emerald set in gold.

As is standard practice, Linda asked Maria if she had experienced healing before and if she had anything specific for us to focus on? Maria smiled, or grimaced, for on her pained face it was hard to define her expression, but her voice was deep and melodic and seemed to hum in the cold air. She told us she had never before heard of our little healing clinic but this week three separate people had mentioned our clinic's name. It was a synchronicity that she felt she had to follow, so voilà, here she was!

With a certain intensity, she looked at us both and seemed to reflect for a moment before asking us if we had ever exorcised demons? Taken aback, Linda answered, "No," and I stuttered something about exorcism not being our role in this healing centre but, forewarned, I closed my eyes and imagined a silver cloak being cast around my whole being as a spiritual protection.

Maria proceeded to tell us her story, how she had been summoned by a Russian oligarch to a house in London to do a psychic drawing of his paternal grandfather. This was not unusual for her as she moved in high circles and was paid exceedingly well for her unusual art skills. She was taken up three flights of stairs and passed through rooms that were lavishly decorated, including a smaller room that was entirely empty apart from a glass coffin with a seemingly naked girl lying prone inside.

She met the Russian in his office room and explained to him that she could only draw a spirit if the spirit chose to present itself to her. The Russian smiled and told her a little of the history of his grandfather. He was a lawyer in Moscow, a sworn advocate for the revolutionaries in the struggles before the fall of the Tsar in 1907. He eventually become a trusted adviser to Lenin and the Bolshevik leaders but was always regarded as a hard man, not to be trifled with.

Maria was given a gold watch to hold, that had once belonged to the grandfather and she was led back downstairs to an area in the dining room where she at once set up her easel and then began to meditate, holding the watch in her hands to help with the attunement into the spirit world. These were her words as best I can recall:

"The old man came to me quickly but he appeared ill at ease, which is unusual. I am not clairaudient so I am unable to listen to their words and rely on my inner vision to partake in detail. Most of my spirit sitters appear to me in grace, seemingly happy to pose but not for too long as it seems to tire them to be connected to our physical plane for more than half an hour, plus I also feel drained if the sitting goes on for too long. This man had a sombre look, a yellow pallor that did not appear healthy; again this surprised me as spirits usually present themselves looking younger, in a healthier state of being.

"I began to draw his outline, letting my hand flow with my mind elsewhere, which is my normal custom. In spirit drawings you try not to think about what you see and let the forces direct your pencil but on this occasion I was minded to refocus on his detail, the way his moustache waved and how his eyebrows were at variance with the lines on his forehead. Then I became aware of another presence far stronger than this grandfather figure. My vision became blurred with a yellow haze and I could hear metallic sounds drumming with a hideous timbre.

"My hand kept sketching but now against my will. I could not stop! The grandfather figure had been cast aside and in his place gradually appeared a foul demon. As well as the evil sounds the smells were noxious, like carrion, or the stink of an abattoir. A foul figure began to emerge to *the side of me, huge, at least nine feet high; male, stripped to the waist, with a shaven skull. His eyes had slit lids that accentuated the white sclera around his black pupils. He had no coloured iris, just this demonic stare with issues of blood seeping forth from every orifice.*

"Engulfed by sheer terror I tried to scream but no sound uttered from my lips as my whole being foundered in dizzy spirals, being slowly sucked into this demon's vile purgatory sphere, drawn by a ghastly magnetic gravitation. The light of our human world was now almost extinguished as I was pulled further and further into a vast dark orb of shadows where this monster awaited me. The stench was unbearable and I knew that my life was about to be curtailed as a victim of this awful apparition.

"High above me I saw this hideous face, which I now recognised as a low-caste Lemurian type, long exiled from Atlantis, exultant as it raised a knife in sheer ecstasy to slice me into pieces.

"Then a rush of pure fragrance and a beam of aqua light flooded into this repulsive underworld and the Lemurian was cast into ash as I was swept up by a winged figure, Azrael, or perhaps another mighty angel and I basked in the pure love and security of his beautiful arms, my trauma now left far behind me.

"As a recompense, he released some of my past lives for me to see in some detail; I looked back in time and saw myself cast in Nero's court attending the beautiful Mercedes, a courtesan harlot trapped in Nero's chambers. She contained within her the great Christ soul of the Master known as Jesus but he had now forsaken his

connection with the Adonai as he commenced upon his forty oblatory lives in the wilderness of our subterranean world, always suffering as he absorbed and exorcised the evil as he cleansed the lower heavens.[25] In other lives I saw myself loved, incarnating both as male and female, tortured, worshipped, burnt as a pagan but in truth always aspiring towards a higher consciousness. Then with my heart pounding with tremendous love for this beautiful divine being I found myself cascading back down into my human psyche.

"As I recovered my pulverised senses, I heard a furore around me. I opened my eyes to find I had fallen from my stool and lay in a heap upon the rich Persian carpet. The Russian's aides fussed around me and gingerly helped me back to my feet as the oligarch himself stood nearby looking entranced at my unfinished drawing of his grandfather. I apologised to the suzerain explaining I had lost my connection and had fainted from exhaustion but he enthused at my drawing saying I had captured the essence of his grandfather's power. He turned the drawing around and to my amazement there were two completed figures not one!

"The now familiar grandfather peered towards the onlooker, looking determined in a grim manner, but behind him and also somehow exuding from deep within the old lawyer, stood a menacing bald cossack, like a humanised version of my hated Lemurian. The cossack looked macabre, with a threatening sabre sword in his right hand. I was astonished! My own hand had created these figures whilst my spirit had been swept away into a dark underworld.

"My assignment completed, I gathered my art materials and sheepishly left the building with my payment doubled. I crept home with both the vision of Heaven and Hell resounding within me."

Maria paused at this point in her story saying how she had suffered several sleepless nights, so terrifying had been her demon ordeal. She now asked us for healing to help replenish her energies and lay in repose on the couch, requesting off-body healing of at least twelve inches; she was most specific about the imperial measurement.

Then Linda and I passed our hands around Maria's energy points, channelling light and love, pausing where we found tiny torrents of energy leaking from her etherial body. Then caressing high above her chakras, calling upon angels to heal this special lady's spiritual wounds.

Later, when Maria slipped away from the clinic she said she could now flow back into her daily life with her spiritual scars healed and anew.

By chance, a few months later, I came across Maria's book of poems and inner visions.[26] Her book confirmed to me that she was indeed a holy lady but her gift of clairvoyance was a mixed blessing, for every sighting of a beautiful object was seemingly eclipsed by a vision of an awful entity, or foul creature. Clearly, Maria had exemplary writing skills as well as her extraordinary artistic gifts and I found myself being drawn into her surreal inner world, in particular being fascinated by her written description of the horse-men who sometimes guarded her at night.

She described how a winged centaur had stood beside her bed at night protecting her from some unnamed horror and when the danger had passed the centaur had shot off through her closed window like an arrow aimed at the stars.

Maria's description hearkened me back in time to my classroom in Gravesend, when little Johnny told his class peers that he had seen a centaur walk through the garden fence. You could have heard a pin drop for it was about as close to holy reverence you will ever find in a Year Three classroom but Johnny did not mention the word centaur, as it was not in his limited vocabulary. He said he had seen a big horse with a man's head and arms. There was no mention of a bow and arrow, or spear. He simply said the horse man had looked at him for a while before disappearing through the fence. Johnny did not appear fazed by the actual centaur but was truly astonished that it had walked through the fence rather than jump over the top. After a reverent hush of about ten seconds another child eagerly seized the opportunity to chip in with his own 'Show and Tell' story and the centaur spell was broken. But when two months later Johnny's mother died with a progressive cancer I wondered whether his centaur vision was a kind of sad premonition, or warning.

Back in the day centaurs were regarded by the Greeks as being wild, sensuous, with an uncontrolled passion for life. Indeed they have been described as 'The Hell's Angels' of Greek mythology.[27]

Yet Chiron, half-brother to Zeus, was a fondly remembered wise centaur, famous for both his healing powers and for tutoring many legendary mythical figures including Ajax, Jason, Perseus, Achilles and Hercules. Chiron had a most dignified end to his life on earth after exchanging his immortality with Prometheus and being granted a constellation in the stars, with Sagittarius being named in his honour.

In more recent times the centaur has become frequently associated with humanistic psychology as being half-human and half-horse.[28] The centaur neatly represents a union between the mental faculties and physical well-being. People who are too mind-orientated feel as if they are 'out of their body' and quest in their transpersonal therapy to become whole again with 'centaur consciousness'.

Back in the 1970s, my spiritual teacher taught me that the horse was a recognised occult symbol for the higher mind (with the donkey/ass representing the lower mind). I think he would be fascinated to hear that the centaur now represented a higher form of consciousness in modern psychology. But I personally will always regard the centaur as an angelic being.

EIGHT

Matrix Magic and Lucid Dreaming

NOW RETIRED, OR semi-retired, I could accompany Carol on her jaunts across Europe to do her specialist courses such as Matrix Energetics. I had no great desire to learn quantum healing but it was fun to travel with Carol to Germany to meet her rather magical friends. They would spend the day cooped up in a conference hall whilst I floated around beautiful Kirchzarten on a hired bicycle. In the evenings we would meet in a restaurant to marvel at the day's events, when sometimes matrix miracles did actually happen, whereby the lame would cast off their shackles and walk, nay run around the stage.

Little Lorne was unable to run or even walk anymore, not since her sudden fall on that cold February day. Her tears trickled upon the downtrodden paving stone like a blessing. In pity, the granite revealed its hidden mystery to the stricken girl, opening her eyes to a myriad of sparkling prisms. In wonder Lorne gazed at this secret universe and quite forgot her pain.

"Poliomyelitis," her Doctors explained to her shocked parents, "with meningitis complications. She will never walk again."

Days passed on by with Lorne listening for friendly footsteps but only the masked nurses entered her quarantined domain. Then she was turned and trussed like a doll. How Lorne longed to slip back into time and skip with her friends or run free through the green meadows. "Why me?" she cried but her anguished parents were unable to answer. Like many children, before and after her, she and her friends had played with contaminated water trickling from a sewer pipe and now they had to pay such an awful price.

Her fevered mind focused on the ceiling cracks, creating shapes that danced or flew like fairies in front of her. Uprisen, these shapes took on a form of their own and whispered inside her head, "Oh you will walk again, you will!"

The Doctors shook their heads but now revived the words became Lorne's mantra: "I will walk again, I will!" And to everyone's astonishment she did, in time casting away both her leg irons and walking frame. But why did this little girl have to suffer such sorrow? Was it to feel the pain, to ignite her soul, so that she would later become a portal of hope for others who had forsaken their own soul's journey and had become lost in despair?

◈

Lorne explained to me why she was sometimes a 'reluctant medium'. Her main income was running her guest house, which was renowned for being a haven for fairies. The fairy folk probably thrived on Lorne's particular brand of vibration and love and allowed themselves to be seen by her. House guests with clairvoyant or clairsentient attributes might also see or sense the fairies flying around her house like little darting fuchsias.

Running her guest house business was tiring enough but Lorne also made time to formally sit as a medium, serving people who might need to contact spirit. These sittings she could cope with but sometimes spirit would connive to complicate her life, leaving her feeling exhausted as if on the edge of chaos.

As an example Lorne explained how one evening she went shopping at her local superstore but afterwards found that her car had been stolen. Already tired and rattled after a busy day, Lorne had to attend the nearby police station and was shown into the interview room by two burly policemen. However, before she could give them details about her missing car, spirit intervened and Lorne was compelled to give both policemen messages about their recently departed loved ones, which resulted in both men being reduced to tears, one sobbing at the detail given to him. What should have taken about fifteen minutes to formally record a crime, took over an hour before the men could sufficiently recover their poise. The suspicion remained that spirit had arranged for the car to be stolen so that Lorne would have to visit the police station to speak with the bereaved policemen! The happy outcome was that Lorne's car was recovered undamaged the next day.

At the healing clinic I listened as Glyn sat back in his chair and spoke of his unhappy childhood. Taking shallow breaths to avoid a deeper connection to his emotions he described the sorrowful seven-year-old child inside who blamed himself for his parents' divorce. As he spoke my feelings slowly morphed into his and I was also cast back in time, feeling his pain like a surrogate parent.

The sofa in my grandparents' house became my womb as I fled within, creeping under the covers, reeling from the court's ruling that I had to be separated from my mother. There were so many tears that I was completely unable to see when my nana finally plucked me out of the sofa, a heartbroken sob of a child. Pneumonia soon set in to delay the switch to my paternal home, for I did not want to live anymore, for how could I live without my mum?

In time I learnt to mask my emotions and tagged along in the company of Geoff and caring nana

Bertha and soon pitied poor disabled granddad Ted. Too early I was awakened to life's painful lessons of cause and effect. For years I dwelt in a void, frozen as if wrapped in a dream. How does one repair the damage of those fatal blows when torn between both parents with the courts pronouncing you can choose only one?

Glyn's tale mirrored mine to a certain extent. He said he had no emotion left, no love to give. It was all frozen deep within, far away.

Observing Glyn's struggle to cope with his deep depression, I wondered if he could blank out his anger forever? Would he find a way to free himself from his self-imposed torture, or would he end up slitting his wrists somewhere in a lonely bedsit?

When she said, "You flow like water"
Her words made a little splash
way down inside of me.
Like a stone being thrown
into a deep dark sea.

Then she said, "You are a natural healer,
That people liked to be with me,
for my stillness calmed their hyperactivity."
But my doubts kicked in and I wondered
if this were true or if she was just kidding me.

For a period of about two weeks I experienced lucid dreams whilst in the process of awakening from my night sleep. In my half sleep I would see a screen, about the size of an iPad, with a vivid scene being portrayed. It was like watching a film clip but like many dreams it made no sense to me. As my mind kicked in the lucid dream would fade away and I would be left in wonder at what I had seen.

Success came easily to Ivan. He was a mathematical whizz at his grammar school, good at sports and a popular choice for Head Boy. He studied accountancy at university and became a corporate high flier in the world of finance. Rather oddly, none of this made him feel complete as he always achieved for other people, especially his family, friends and college tutors.

Ivan wanted to understand himself better and felt led to explore his dream world, thinking that dreams are a way to reveal the unconscious mind. By using mnemonically induced lucid dreaming techniques Ivan began to explore his dreams, commanding himself to recall his dreams in detail. At night he would gaze to his upper left-hand side to visualise a screen and then paused until his unconscious mind created visions on the screen. In a kind of half sleep Ivan would watch absorbed as figures and scenes unfolded before his eyes.

On the first occasion there was a river scene in bright sunlight with people he did not recognise. They were in party mode, sunbathing and messing about spraying water on each other. Whenever Ivan tried to analyse what he was seeing the vision would quickly fade as his conscious mind interfered with the unconscious messages he was receiving.

Ivan was fascinated by what he was seeing but unclear about its meaning. He began to go to bed earlier at night but did not always succeed in creating a lucid dream for if he tried too hard his unconscious mind would not co-operate.

Over the weeks that followed a pattern emerged. He would see places, get a glimpse of a foreign map from somewhere like the old Yugoslavia and be shown a train or bus ticket but he could not understand the writing or destination on the ticket. It was all rather obscure. Sometimes a blonde middle-aged woman would reappear and in time she gradually became more prominent in his night visions.

At work people began to notice a change in Ivan for he had become more withdrawn, indeed a little sullen. He was no longer the life and soul of a party but rather a reluctant participant. If they had stepped inside Ivan's head they would have realised that he was now obsessed with finding this mysterious blonde woman of his lucid dreams.

Then one night Ivan's spiritual exploration moved into a new dimension for he somehow effortlessly morphed into the familiar scene that he had been passively observing for weeks on end. This was a whole new experience for he could now feel the breeze on his skin and listen to the sparrows chirping in the trees as he slowly followed the blonde lady in front of him. He could feel the soft grass under his feet but he did not feel as if he were in his physical body.

The pond in front of him was shaped like a heart and the park somehow appeared familiar to him. He passed by a table with a young couple sipping coffee and chatting together as young lovers do. They were not speaking in English but Ivan recognised the accent. It was Romanian with a Hungarian dialect, but what astonished him was that he knew what they were saying. He could understand this Romanian language.

He followed the blonde lady as she slowly walked towards the park gates. She seemed distressed and took several big gasps of air before she left the park. A sign indicated, Larcul Balauruli and Ivan somehow knew that he was in the province of Timisoara, a town on the west side of Romania.

The woman walked along the main road and then turned into a side street. Ivan followed about twenty paces behind. He knew this street. It was familiar to him. In fact he knew where this woman was going. He could see the large, dark, three-storey house on the other side of the road and sure enough the blonde lady crossed the road, entered the gate and walked up the steps to the house. She pulled out her keys from a black leather purse and entered the building. She had not noticed Ivan following behind her.

Ivan stood in the road outside the house and looked up at the bedroom window at the top of the house. The curtains seemed to move as if beckoning him to enter and Ivan felt *compelled to move up the steps. He did not need a key. He simply walked through the door. It was an odd feeling as if he had passed through vapour. Then he trudged up the stairs until he reached the third flight.*

The door was open so he stepped into the room and peered through the gloom at an old lady lying propped up in her bed. She was in repose, with her eyes closed. She seemed to be struggling to breathe. Ivan tried to take her hand but it just passed on through her and he now fully realised he was in spirit form. Nevertheless he could feel the tears fall from his eyelids for he knew that this lady was his wife from his past life. She was in pain and was probably dying but there was nothing he could do or say to help her.

But then she awoke and seemed to sense his presence. Her pained face at once broke into a smile as she gazed in his direction with light in her eyes. "Oh Gregor, are you there? Have you come to visit me? I've missed you so much. I don't want to live anymore. I just want it all to end."

At this point the blonde woman came into the room with a drink in her hand. She comforted her mother and wiped her perspiring forehead. The old lady sipped from her glass and then settled back on her pillow. She closed her eyes and fell back into a troubled sleep. Ivan knew that she would not wake up, that her life felt complete and that she was now ready to move on to other spheres. Somehow he had been able to comfort her by his presence. Perhaps to indicate that there was a life beyond the secular world that she inhabited.

Then he felt himself falling away from this strangely familiar house in a Romanian suburb. He was spinning, dizzily travelling back in time until he felt himself land with a gentle bump back in his bed and then he slept, now fully removed from his lucid dreaming.

When I look at beautiful gems, such as a ruby, sapphire or emerald, I see beyond the trapped light in its golden casing and know how this light once shone as part of our planet's Elohim and may even be part of a crystallised human soul that fell from spirit into matter so many billions of years ago.

When he was alone, it was always harder for the visionary to fight against his astral persecutors. He described to us how one sunny day he strolled along the Kew Gardens towpath, breathing deeply, trying to lift his spirits away from the terrible oppression that he felt for mankind. It was mid-day and he was perturbed to feel waves of terror once again sweeping over him. Surely he was safe in this beautiful sunlit environment? He stopped and shook in fear at the horrors he saw in front of him. Once again the siren voices whispered into his left ear, this time urging him to throw himself into the river, to commit suicide. The astral voices said he was worthless, an utter waste of space. The river looked inviting It would be an easy way to end his suffering.

Panic-stricken, yet frozen for he could not move his arms or legs, he had to will himself to take but a step, to fight against these evil forces who could somehow control his body movements. It took all his will-power to ease his foot forward an inch. Very slowly, with the inner voices shrieking with rage, he gradually edged away from the river towards a nearby park bench. Then he collapsed upon the seat and withdrew into himself and waited until at last his astral tormentors left him alone.

NINE

Meditation, Dreams and Astral Attacks

CAROL AND I had been to Germany to meditate in Mother Meera's Darshan in Balduinstein. The whole trip had been a lovely experience. Sitting in silence for two hours with our fellow meditators, although challenging, had been blissful. We were keen to attend a meditation group in our local area, aspiring to help bring love and light into our troubled world. We discovered a meditation group that was starting in our local library. On the given day there was an excellent attendance of approximately forty people, mainly women, who all sat on chairs, in a circle with candles burning on the floor. It looked quite sublime. I quickly gathered it was a Mindfulness, Buddhist type of meditation.

After a delay for late entrants, we began with everyone stating their name and doing a 'weather report' on their feelings. "I'm Muriel and I am feeling a bit cloudy today." After hearing all sorts of childlike weather reports I simply stated my name and said I was feeling fine. Carol said something about being stormy.

Eventually the meditation started and we were instructed every ten seconds or so on what to do: "Breathe into your tummy." "Listen to your breathing." "Watch your thoughts but don't try to stop them."

After about ten minutes of this meditation instruction we opened our eyes to find one of the ladies shaking uncontrollably. She said she had been feeling very tense and doing the deep breathing had led to a catharsis of some sort. She slipped down onto the floor with her head resting on someone's handbag. We watched fascinated as she shook from head to toe, totally unable to stop her body from shaking. "It's happened before," she said in an anguished voice.

After caring for the stricken lady on the floor the group leader pressed on with the meditation. We were told to sit up and not rest with our back to the chairs. We were given more breathing advice; after taking a deep breath we had to hold it for a few seconds before breathing out. Then we were instructed to ignore any noises we could hear in the street. After several more similar directions we opened our eyes again to discuss how we felt. "Did we feel more relaxed?" Apparently many people did.

This discussion eventually petered out so we were off again, led into a guided meditation whereby we were walked across a field and admired the sky and some wild flowers by the side of the path. I quite like guided meditations but usually struggle to 'see' what I am meant to see. By now I was fed up with being told how to sit, breathe and think and evidently Carol felt the same so we both quietly slipped away into the night.

Evidently I did not channel much light into the world on this occasion but TM meditators have proven that group meditation can successfully bring peace and calm to troubled areas; so long may they do so.

My mother explained her own personal meditation technique and emphasised that she did not try to <u>do</u> anything. She simply sat in her chair and relaxed, sending her genuine love thoughts over to a beautiful Japanese ornamental tree that graced her presence nearby.

She loved this tree for the sway of its branches in the wind and how the sunlight flickered through the dancing leaves, and during her meditation she thanked the tree for its beauty and grace. Then with her eyes closed she moved her attention away from her mind to her heart centre and waited for the feeling of absolute peacefulness to engulf her. It was only later when she returned to the present moment and opened her eyes from her blissful meditation that she realised that although she had done nothing, the tree had actually embraced her with its love, not the other way round. She said that all trees and flowers had this ability to love humankind, if only we would allow this to happen.

He had been forewarned that this ordeal was coming. It was all part of the visionary's redemptive process, whereby evil entities were attracted to him like moths to a flame and somehow he transmuted them into light. It was his life's work.

Now it was long past midnight. He had pleaded with my mother to stay with him to help him survive the astral onslaught and with reluctance she agreed. She sat next to him and felt the atmosphere in the room change. It became icy cold and threatening, as if a violent storm had broken into the room.

She watched as terror swept over him in waves. He appeared unable to block it out. It was as if he had to absorb the evil elements as they attacked him. Objects started to move around and drop to the floor. Sweat poured off the visionary's face as the entities repeatedly attacked him. She held him close to her, whispering words of comfort; trying to keep his mind strong and focused in the here and now. Somehow they held on together during this astral onslaught, like survivors clasping onto a lifeboat, until at last dawn came and the evil spell that had been cast over them broke and together they escaped into the coming day.

Carol and I had also suffered astral attacks on a fairly regular basis. They always occurred at night, often at the point of sleep but we never had them at the same time. They were terrifying: imagine a buzz saw grinding into your head and you will get some idea of the ordeal. Strangely, you could not just wake up from the noise because physically you were totally frozen as if paralysed. I was barely able to utter a sound but Carol would sometimes whimper and rock around in bed in obvious distress. I would then wake up and hold her hand and the attack would then quite quickly dissipate but you could still feel the presence of an entity in the room.

When the attacks first happened to me I tried to fight back against the 'buzz saw', but you really are rendered helpless, unable to move or scream. The entity was just too dominant and very, very frightening because you feel as if you are going to be driven mad. I was given advice to avoid confronting the entity and instead withdraw within. Then I imagined myself holding onto a giant cross deep inside of me and I found that I was then safe and secure. In retrospect it is hard to gauge but I think the attacks lasted for about ten minutes or so but they would always leave you feeling exhausted and shaking in terror. We wondered why we had these attacks and who would be the cause of them?

After experiencing these astral attacks for several years, I casually mentioned them to my father who was on one of his visits to see us and his grandchild. I described in some detail how terrifying they were. My father listened acutely and from that day onward we never had another attack. I now surmise that Geoffrey was astral travelling at night, trying to read our minds, or trying to find something out about us. It is just a pity he did not try phoning us more often!

Annie's aunt Jean had never married and thought that life had somehow passed her by. She was a plain child, a honeymoon baby, not really wanted by her parents who had hoped for a strong boy, not a girl who cried a lot and had finicky ways.

Her childhood and schooling had been badly disrupted by the war years. She spent almost two years evacuated in different lodgings in North Devon. She hated being stuck in the countryside with her mother and was totally devastated to hear that her best friend Pamela, whose parents had opted to stay in London, had been killed when a bomb dropped on their house in the London suburbs of Lee Green. This had an overbearing effect upon her, for Jean somehow blamed herself for surviving the second world war when her friend had died. She never really recovered from this shock and forever after suffered post-traumatic stress disorder.

On leaving school she served time working in typing pools for big companies but she always suffered from depression and never found a proper career to give her a purpose in life. She lived in rented accommodation and drank to release her dark feelings, becoming alcohol dependent by her mid-forties. The men who drifted in and out of her life never understood her dark malady and bitter ironic humour. She did not love herself so it was hard for Jean to accept love from these men.

When her parents died Jean became more or less adrift from her natural family but she did keep in touch with her sister's youngest child Annie who had been the one bright light in her life. Annie was everything that Jean was not; she was wanted and loved by her parents and was a pretty, talented child with a caring nature. On the rare occasions when Jean was asked to care for Annie, the child would soon make her smile by her jaunty manner and then astound her with her artistic skills. When little, Annie would give her auntie unconditional love, holding onto her leg and gazing up at her with her beautiful blue eyes and saying, "I love you, Auntie Jean." Hearing these heartfelt words nearly broke Jean's heart.

Now in her fifties, Jean did occasional shop work, or cleaning but gradually became dependent on benefits to pay her rent. She took anti-depressants to try to get by and at a particularly low point in her life thought there was no point in living so she downed a handful of barbiturates and sat back in her chair waiting for the end to come. After two hours she started vomiting and felt so terribly ill that she phoned her sister for help and was duly rushed to hospital to have her stomach pumped. For the next two weeks she felt excruciating pain throughout her body and vomited all the time.

After this narrow escape from death Jean was allocated a social worker and for several months had to report in each day to describe her feelings. The social worker supported Jean as best she could and persuaded a housing trust to offer Jean accommodation in West London, so she moved into a little studio flat in Brentford. The Brentford streets were anything but salubrious but in about twenty minutes Jean could march over Kew Bridge, marvel at the beauty of the River Thames and for two pence would gain entry into Kew Gardens. Sitting amongst the foliage and flowers Jean felt at peace. It was one of the few joys in her life.

Her other love was alcohol, red or white wine, or cider, she did not really mind what she drank. It was as if she were escaping from a sense of guilt that her dear childhood friend had died but she had somehow survived the war years. When her mind returned to that dark place she became overwhelmed by depression.

Life was now a drudgery. She hated her cleaning jobs, especially when she had to rise at dawn to clean office buildings and she fell out with her sister who tired of her cadging and hysterical behaviour, especially when hopelessly inebriated. So it was Annie, now a mum herself, who fielded the desperate phone calls, the black despair flooding down the phone lines whilst Jean wept, so ashamed of burdening her niece.

A few years passed but nothing changed for the better so one autumn day Jean decided that she would be a burden no more. She bolted the door to her flat and ingested about twenty paracetamol, mixed with about forty ephedrine tablets. Then she waited for the blackness to engulf her. After an hour her head began to reel with dizziness and *she panicked, phoning Annie to come and save her but Annie was out, unable to respond to her cry for help.*

Hours later the door was smashed open and they found frail Jean dead on the floor covered with vomit. Another victim to loneliness and despair.

After the sparsely attended funeral service at the crematorium, Annie took her aunt's ashes home in a red urn. She placed the urn on her sideboard, alongside a vase of bright flowers. It was a genuine gesture of love for her poor aunt who had been so kind to her as a child. Then she went about her domestic tasks preparing a meal for her ravenous family.

Her two Labrador dogs came bounding into the house from the long garden. They wagged their tails in delight for Annie had been out for most of the day. Then inexplicably they looked startled and stared at Jean's urn on the sideboard. Both dogs started to howl in unison and then whimpered and whined as they slowly backed out of the room. Once out of the house they bolted to the back of the garden and hid under the Birch tree. They refused to enter the house again whilst the ashes were in the house. Nothing could persuade them, so reluctantly Annie removed the ashes and stored the urn in the garage. Only then did the dogs come creeping back into the living room.

The footnote to this sad saga is that a few days later Annie's husband Jeff was busy in the garage topping up the oil levels to his car. Both dogs traipsed into the garage to accompany Jeff and once again they sensed the urn's presence. Again they howled in distress and fled to the back of the garden. Only when the urn was buried deep under the earth did the dogs relax and behave as normal again.

One night I dreamt I was in a park sitting on top of a step-ladder, observing a decaying oak tree. There were some children playing nearby trying to hit a golf ball in the air with a three-iron golf club. Their own merry laughter was at odds with my own despair at the suffering tree. I seemed to be a scientist of sorts, a kind of tree doctor, an arborist perhaps but this tree was rotten to the core so there was little I could do but try to reason why this beautiful tree had decayed so badly.

I closed my eyes and listened, hoping for communication with the spirit of the tree. To do this I had to step out of my scientist persona and turn off my mind, to stay in neutral and not analyse anything. But I could not help but wonder if this tree would be angry with humankind or sad? For it had been established for over two hundred years, doing its work, cleaning the air, providing shelter for a whole variety of creatures and insects and adding considerable beauty to the countryside.

I climbed down my step-ladder and by the trunk of the tree found a rotting branch on the ground. I stroked the bark which fell away to my touch and watched as my fingers started to decompose. The tree was telling me that we were all linked together, that we humans would also suffer from the air pollution.

Anxious, I washed my hands and was relieved to find that my fingers were not damaged.

In my report I would recommend that the trees be sprayed with BT chemicals (*Bacillus thuringiensis var kurstaki*) to rid the trees of the oak moths that infested the weakened trees; but I knew that this interference with nature further impaired the trees, just as vaccination dissipated the overall human immune system. The real solution seemed impossible to achieve: to drastically reduce sulphur output and poisonous factory ozone chemicals being released into the air, for with each passing year these chemicals produced damaging acid rain, which further poisoned the earth.

What is a dream and what is real? Far away a scream is heard in the desert of man's feelings. Eventually a body squirms into action and a face weaves suitable patterns of expression.

Antony stood in his attic gazing at the myriad of paintings gathering grime in the darkness. Depression had gathered over him like dusk. His work of the ages had once again been neglected by the powers that be, who could never understand, or resonate, to his astute cosmic consciousness.

At the back of the attic lay dusty portraits of forgotten models, or long-lost friends and acquaintances. Situated by the near wall attractive landscapes were stacked in untidy neglected bundles. Along the side wall were his notorious animal rights paintings, illustrating how monstrous evil intention actually created the burgeoning diseases that the vivisectors were trying to dispel.

His most treasured paintings, that revealed the development of soul consciousness, were at the forefront of the room, rich in their mystic symbolism; among them the Sea of Galilee, vivid in colour, depicting not the nondescript Lake Tiberias in Israel but the higher magnetic field of the whole of our planet where spiritual thoughts operate.

The Jewish forebears Abraham and Sarah were shown not as original citizens of the Jewish race but as the god/goddess of the sun – restoring the magnetic chromosphere of the Elohim. There were a series of fabulous paintings indicating that Jesus did not spend forty days in a desert wilderness but had to endure forty wretched human lives, often in lowly Gehenna states since his perfect manifestation as a Christ soul living amongst the Nazarenes in Palestine.

Antony knew that the tide of life was running out for him. He had already indicated as much to his friends and had decided to attend the Order on the following Sunday for spiritual replenishment.

On this given day he sat alone in his familiar pew at the back of the sporadic congregation and listened as the ministrant began to speak. The talk was all about love and he opened his heart to the beautiful words of comfort. But later in an unguarded moment an astral lance was plunged into his back and he was mortally wounded on the etheric plane. Somehow he staggered home on the tube gasping for breath.

His adopted son Glen phoned us in a desperate panic. Antony was gravely ill. Would Carol come now! Her homeopathy and healing skills might be able to save him! We drove fast to Kew and ran to the front door but our urgent flight was in vain for we found our spiritual teacher lying in peace upon his bed, without breath and no longer in any discomfort. His lifetime of spiritual work was now complete. With tears in my eyes I kissed his forehead, still warm to the touch but now a pallid grey and we all cried at his suffering and marvelled at his creative accomplishments.

TEN

Esoteric Teaching and a Night Vision

SOMETIMES I WOULD read something in Mr Ferrier's esoteric teachings and be moved to share it with my Christian friends. A case in point is Todd Ferrier's version of 'The Feeding of the Multitude'.[(29)]

In the four Gospels account, Jesus is cast as an alchemist who can turn five barley loaves and two small fishes into enough food to feed five thousand people. It is a miracle and Jesus is presented as a man full of love who cares for the people who turn up in the desert to listen to him. That Jesus was a holy Nazarene and thus a vegetarian, so unlikely to feed via fish is bye the bye, but as Mr Ferrier notes, there is no spiritual element to this story, just a bit of magic to leave one in awe of the personal Jesus.

Now I am no biblical scholar but there seems to me to be enough holes in this story to render it highly unlikely to have been a physical event and one does have to bear in mind that the New Testament was written more than three hundred years after

'Jesus' passed on. Why would the Master travel into the desert to give his teaching to the multitude? There are no mountains in the desert, as it is flat terrain. How did the five thousand people travel there? Why did they not provide food provisions for themselves? Where did the two small fishes come from? After a few hours in the desert heat the fish would almost certainly be 'off' and probably rancid.

Todd Ferrier says it was originally an allegorical story told by Jesus to his disciples. When he spoke to people who were not within his inner circle he always taught by using parables. He had to use basic language because in those days the inner spiritual life was lost, as if in a spiritual desert. He always 'fed' his followers truths through the five senses so that they could better understand what he was trying to teach them. Thus the barley loaves represented the 'bread' of life, being wholesome spiritual truths such as purifying one's life, being kind and loving to each other, avoiding jealousy, hate, exploitation and war. Plus avoiding unnecessary superstitions and making cruel animal sacrifices in the temples.

The fish are not creatures at all but were profound mysteries. Jesus revealed to the masses two small mysteries. Todd Ferrier reveals that they were 'the nature of the soul' and 'the character of the life unto which it was called'.[30]

But the spiritual food given to the masses was not assimilated because people generally did not want to change their lifestyle, for they were too dominated by their sense life to begin a holy trail. So the spiritual food fragments were returned in twelve baskets. Thus meaning the beautiful truths were not lost but were always ready for the soul when the individual concerned was ready to receive them. Twelve relates to the twelve labours, or gates, of the soul.

So I enthusiastically sent this new interpretation to my Baptist friends, wondering if they would discuss the issue with me, but they were adamant that the original story was factual and gloried in the power of the personal Jesus, so Mr Ferrier's little pearls of wisdom were cast away by them, as if they were stones.

I have met people who are fearful that aliens could invade our planet but it would not surprise me if there were already several other representatives from our solar system living on our planet, either as human beings or in the sub-human creature kingdom. Of course there is no firm evidence to back up such a claim but Todd Ferrier indicated that all the people populating the planets before the 'Fall' from spirit into matter were 'human'.[31] This means if we were to meet a passing Uranian, or a Martian, he would be in a recognisable human form, not a blob on legs as aliens are often presented in our science fiction movies. Todd Ferrier also said that no new souls have been created since the fall, so this insinuates that at soul level we are all billions of years old![32]

These days one has to step very carefully when contemplating issues such as race or ethnic groups, but surely it is a mystery why there are so many different races on separate continents including: Caucasoid (European), Negroid (African), Mongoloid (Chinese/Japanese) and Australoid (native Australian/native American). Scientists who investigate issues such as genetics/DNA have found that genetically there is very little separating any of these ethnic groups; quite simply we are all united as human beings. However, science still clings on to the theory that we have all evolved from the apes. Naturally Christian creationists beg to differ and point to Genesis which suggests all races developed from Adam.

It is interesting to glean from Todd Ferrier some further esoteric insights into our planetary history. It is alleged that in a private audience, Mr Ferrier stated that the Chinese (thus the Mongoloid race) were the original inhabitants of the Moon; I have never found this written in his many books, although he does write that the Luna souls are now on the Earth.[33]

It may be of interest that Ancient Chinese emperors worshipped the harvest moon in autumn, as they believed that the practice would bring them a plentiful harvest the following year and even today, following that tradition, there is a season of sharing moon cakes, plus a strange rabbit moon cult called 'Chang'e', known as the goddess of the moon. I would guess that the Inuit (Eskimo) people, Koreans and Japanese could also be included in this 'Chinese' racial grouping.

Also allegedly, Todd Ferrier hinted that the Indian/Asian peoples originated from the planet Venus and that the cow contains the lower souls of fallen Venusians who were unable to return to human form after the Fall. (In the Hindu religion the cow is regarded as a sacred figure.)[34]

Regarding the Earth's own planetary children, Todd Ferrier informs us that before the Fall, there were meant to be twelve 'houses' or dimensions of 'Judah', (Judah being our planet's divine, or soul name). [35] Not all the houses were populated as none of the developing souls had risen much higher than about the ninth degree/house before the Fall disaster intervened and then the human souls became trapped after incarnating in animal/saurian forms, or worse. According to Mr Ferrier, the surviving houses, or tribes, of Judah are now said to be set in the West and he is scathing of western culture in general because of our over-indulgence in materialism and sensual pleasure. By contrast, Mr Ferrier wrote that the 'Eastern peoples' were spiritually a thousand years ahead of the West.

Mr Ferrier writes at length about the other figures and tribes who have lived and may still be living on our planet. The House of Ephraim are named as the mass of 'young' celestial angels who accompanied the 'minor god' Abaddon, who became the great betrayer, known as the 'Angel of destruction', leading astray Lucifer our angel of the outermost sphere and ultimately persuading the young planetary 'Earth' souls to abandon their devotion to the Divine and instead become bewitched to a love of sensual pleasure and material things.[36]

It would not be a surprise if many of our politicians, judges, bankers and wealthy families were once souls from the House of Ephraim, as they still have an ongoing lust for power and wealth.

By contrast the celestial souls who were originally the teachers of the planetary children and naïvely, out of love, followed the human souls, even into saurian forms in a bid to save them, will always aspire to a higher spiritual consciousness. Sometimes great leaders such as Gandhi and Martin Luther King will lead nations out of their shackles and at other times whole communities of celestial souls have gathered together, as in Ancient Greece.

On a similarly related theme, Todd Ferrier stated that after the fall of Atlantis, which was part of the later fall of our world into matter, the Lemurians who had populated Atlantis entered into one of the fallen spheres and helped to create the occult plane as we know it today. One can surmise that the Lemurians and Atlanteans incarnated into both Egyptian and Mayan communities, which is why there are so many extraordinary monuments, such as precise pyramid structures, that are simply 'out of this world' for their point in time.[37]

Todd Ferrier's remarkable teaching is regarded by his devotees both as our planet's 'soul history' and as a kind of template for celestial souls to recover their high consciousness. Sadly few people will ever discover this momentous message because they restrict their soul searching by either sticking with an inflexible religious belief, or live an unspiritual life focused on acquiring money, wealth and over-indulging their senses. Fortunately, in the twenty-first century, people can often choose or devise for themselves their own belief system and not be fixed by a rigid church, or nationalistic dogma, as in previous eras.

"The natural healing force within each of us is the greatest force in getting well."(38) This famous Hippocrates quote is an aphorism for Carol, who had spent most of her working life attempting to heal herself after witnessing verbal and physical violence in her household as a child and then suffering physical damage to her neck and spine as a student at her osteopathic college.

Comparatively recently, one Friday morning Carol woke up to find she was blind in her left eye. She remembered turning awkwardly in her sleep and felt her neck click. We went directly to our local hospital which had an emergency eye unit but after a frustrating day of agonising delay were re-referred to Moorfields Eye Hospital for an appointment on Saturday morning. Poor Carol was an absolute wreck.

At Moorfields Carol was eventually diagnosed as having a dual tear in her retina. It was a serious injury and had to be operated on straight away. There was an eighty per cent chance of success, so with considerable trepidation Carol agreed to the operation. The surgeon was pleased with his operation, whereby he repaired the two tears and fixed the floating retina to her eyeball but Carol then had to wait a fortnight for the outcome.

However, during the following week Carol noticed fluids leaking into the side of her eye. She returned to Moorfields to be told that some fluids had seeped under the retina, an unusual circumstance. The Professor recommended that the retina now have laser treatment to repair this fault. Once again this operation was done on the same day as this diagnosis, with Carol back in a state of shock.

Convinced that her retina eye condition had been caused by her old neck injury, Carol revisited her cranial osteopath to see if he could help her. The cranial osteopath, I will call him Paul, reminded her that he had predicted that she would 'collapse' six months ago, basing this prediction on Carol's penchant for over-running on adrenaline for far too long, so he was not at all surprised by Carol's current affliction.

A good cranial practitioner can read body language/ spines rather like a palmist reads lines on a palm, so by using his biodynamic reasoning Paul could interpret how Carol's spinal compensation patterns eventually led to her head membrane becoming overstretched and thus damaging her left eye – for her eye was at the end of this particular meridian line.

Whilst working on Carol's cranial patterns, clairsentient Paul could 'sense' a little figure hunched up in a foetal position, terrified and holding her tensions locked up inside of her. Indeed this was Carol's early experience of life witnessing the verbal and physical violence in her parents' house.

Following her cranial treatments Carol started having extraordinary Kundalini episodes whereby her body and limbs would shake uncontrollably. It was as if Kundalini Shakti energies were flowing along Carol's subtle body pathways, often moving in different directions, releasing the tensions that had been dormant for so long.

When contemplating a 'cure', the layman will nearly always focus on the physical issue but there are several 'bodies' that have to be considered, including the outer physical/etheric/emotional/mental/astral/

celestial.(39) It is commonplace for people to block out mental or emotional pain by using drugs like anti-depressants but sometimes healing has to take place on several levels before the individual is fully cured. Indeed illness quite often appears to create balance for the soul and the sufferer will have to review many aspects of their life that have been suppressed.

In Carol's case it appears that her eye condition is part of an ongoing process to repair old emotional and physical wounds as she aspires to her ultimate goal of spiritual fulfilment.

After an amazing vision I went to Bastia to see if she could divine what had happened to me. The oracle held my hands. She closed her eyes and cast her light upon the shadows. She saw the healers inside the hospital as they desperately sought to resuscitate the fallen avatar, as she lay prone in intensive care; her heart was now controlled by a life support machine. Threads of wire scattered across her body causing the monitors to beep in despair.

Klara herself was no longer in her body but watched with curiosity as the healers sought in vain to bring vibrancy to her now closed chakras but life's tide had by now almost run out and there was no fetching her back. In the corner of the room, beyond the human eye, an angel prepared to care for the fallen prodigy.

Later at midnight the life support machine was switched off and Klara was finally released from her devastated body. She basked in her freedom and entered the dreams of her beloved ones.

Then she moved south and hoisted the dozing seeker from his slumbers, raising him up and further up, until he found himself resting in a white waiting room. This is the place where the fatally injured have their spiritual wounds healed after their mortal turmoil.

His eyes set upon a ceiling fan but just as he thought nothing was about to happen the fan seemed to open out into a portal and through the opening whirled amazing hieroglyphics. They were in 3D form, absolutely beautiful, with colours and shapes that were entirely new to him. The seeker was aware that he, like the biblical Ezekiel, was being shown the secrets of the planet but they were in a form that his mind had no key to understand. He watched in wonder as these wheels within wheels gradually faded away only to be replaced by an even greater vision. He was mesmerised by their sheer beauty but unable to discern what they represented. It was simply the majesty of God in all his/her glory. After another short passage of time the final hieroglyphics were revealed and then the seeker found himself back in bed, totally humbled by what he had been given to see.

Bastia smiled and said that the avatar had been determined to show us that she was very much alive on a higher sphere and wanted to share the sheer beauty of heaven and how even those with little faith would be enraptured by the boundless love that they would receive.

ELEVEN

The Way of Being

FOR THIS CONCLUDING chapter, I have been thinking about the important events in my life, contemplating the various 'keys' that I have found to direct me in both my inner and outer life. The big question being, are we meant to search for these 'keys' or wait until they present themselves to us?

The notion of keys opening doors is an age-old analogy but a useful one. We are all bound on a path to find work and form relationships and to maybe create families. This is our outer life, where we are seen for what we do and achieve. We are often gauged by our peers by how much money we earn, by our physical appearance and material trophies such as our house, or car. In many ways it is an illusion but whether we like it or not our outer accomplishments are usually evaluated far more highly than any of our worthy inner virtues.

As a young rebel it went entirely against the grain for me to study at college to pass the examinations necessary to enter the field of education. This turned out to be a vital key for me, as teaching SEN children has been a most joyful and natural career, as well as financially rewarding. In my case I needed a goal that really appealed to me before I could study hard to pass the exams.

I am guessing that before we are born we are given a template to follow as best we can, with parents carefully chosen and then it is up to us to develop as life's opportunities present themselves to us. This is our way of being. Finding out who you are and then being yourself is an important part of our quest. As my pop star hero Kevin Ayers once succinctly said, 'Know yourself and be there.'

Our individual karma determines the given template and a few individuals may even carry the burden of a national, or even world karma, which makes life particularly difficult for them. Just being yourself might appear to be an easy process but it is not, for we can easily become lost on our given pathway, a victim to a whole array of addictions, including materialism. Perhaps the addictions themselves are part of our pathway, or karma, but I tend to think they are siren voices leading us astray, like a substitute for divine consciousness. We even call our hard liquor 'spirits'! We need to be wary of allowing our sense life to dominate us. It is a lesson!

Then there is the whole concept of predestination. We all have our birthday but do we also have a given death-day when we are meant to depart from the mortal coil? Do drugs, surgery, or even prayers and healing interfere with this specific death-day, or is this all taken into account?

When my father was called up for the army he bemused his fellow conscripted soldiers by stating that the war would end on his birthday. Although he was just nineteen years of age Geoffrey was already very much in league with the spirit world. You can imagine the mockery he received from his army pals but three years later, to everyone's amazement, he was proved right. Was Geoffrey's spirit guide seeing a predestination pattern of real-life events or was it a lucky guess?

People like to avoid uncertainty as much as possible by taking control of their lives whenever they can. They insure themselves against incidents that will often be out of their control, like accidents or serious illness, but sometimes events happen that are way beyond our control. I was four-and-a-half when my parents split. All my toddler sensibilities were knocked for six and I nurtured a sense of distrust for authority figures which definitely affected my schooling. That was how I responded to this major event but of course other children would and do react quite differently.

Similarly, when I was attacked by a demon I was totally out of any control. I had no defence whatsoever. People may think this episode in my life fanciful but it was incredibly real to me and to this day I am in wonder at the sheer beauty of my angelic rescuer. The incident begs the question, was it meant to be? Did the demon detach itself from me? Did I have a role in creating it? I do not know the answers but I basked in the angelic consciousness of my saviour and now long to return to that magnificent feeling of love and enlightenment.

You can be stuck in your ways and then something can happen, out of the blue as it were, and life is never the same again. My mother was such a case. She worked as a public relations secretary for a big brewery company. She loved her job and enjoyed the esteem of her senior position but this persona was always at odds with the mystic seeker within. At weekends she would be exploring mystic/occult groups in her never-ending search for a truth that resonated for her. After one deep yoga breath too many she was never the same again, cast off into a highly psychic consciousness that she actually found most disturbing. She was unable to work in big business again. The recompense for her being that within a year she finally found the mystic teachings that she had been searching for. Once she read Todd Ferrier's *The Logia* her long search was over and she settled down to enjoy her inner growth. Today she is a most wise and contented ninety-year-old, in wonder at what she has learnt and experienced in her lifetime.

I have written about how people move on through life in these outer spheres as if they were spiritually asleep. Generally speaking, they are unaware of the light within and consequently may well deny the importance of any spiritual life. I am taught that this is because they are heavily veiled. In particular, Todd Ferrier writes about the veil of blood and how it restricts spiritual development. I am of course mindful that there are many beautiful caring souls, including the Dalai Lama, who do eat meat or fish and they seem unaffected by this veil of blood. However, Todd Ferrier has made it very clear that one needs to purify as much as possible in order to attain high consciousness.[(40)]

It was meant to be that I had a mother who led a vegetarian lifestyle, with compassion for the creatures, had nature cure ideals and a determination to locate a spiritual teaching that suited her mystic vision. So at birth, without any effort on my part, I had the veil of blood lifted from me. Perhaps surprisingly, I have never been tempted to eat animal products as my vegetarian diet has always suited my way of being.

In addition, I have never been vaccinated, which I feel not only interferes with one's natural life-force but is based on the evil doctrine of vivisection upon animals. Incidentally, I have never had any allergies, or respiratory, or neurological conditions, from which many of my friends/colleagues have suffered: (hayfever, pet allergies, migrane, asthma etc.) or any metabolic conditions such as diabetes.

I know I fly in the face of popular opinion but I really do think that when science intervenes in the natural circumstances of child development, then there is a price to pay. For example, if you take the MMR combination of vaccinations you may not get measles but you may have some other kind of reaction. At one extreme, I have taught children who suffered strokes after reacting badly to a measles jab. One was left with a withered arm. Parents in the autistic field are frequently convinced that their otherwise healthy baby completely switched off after receiving a vaccination and was never the same again. These autistic cases are very hard to verify but they are a warning. In my view vaccinations are yet another veil over our sensibilities. We should be purifying both our bodies and our environment not poisoning them.

Unusually, my grandparents on both sides of my family were spiritualists (but not my grandfather Ted). As a young man I avoided the Spiritualist Church because I had heard so many stories about 'spirit' giving advice that all sounded quite shallow and meaningless to me. It did not help that my father would step aside from his normal quiet demeanour and thunder around as if he were demented whenever he stepped into his clairvoyant/healer guise. Watching my father flip into an alternative persona was disturbing both to me and my family but when I eventually began my healing course I was pleasantly surprised to find many spiritualists who were most sincere and who set about their healing skills in a gentle and loving manner. Nevertheless I think I will always be wary of channelling spirit entities that can be harmful. For this reason going into trance is a no-go area for me, even though I hear that trance healing can be most powerful.

The 'veil of idolatry' slogan sounds odd in our modern times, for the church has lost much of its power over the general public. However, surely it is inappropriate for church-goers to worship 'Jesus', a human being, albeit a wonderful manifestation of divine love, instead of God? The same applies to Krishna and I am sure that the Buddha would be appalled by the personal worship of him by his followers.

Perhaps a more recognisable form of idolatry is the adulation we heap on pop and film stars and we may even idolise philosophers or even politicians for a short period of time. The wise part of me knows that idolatry is all a nonsense for we need to seek within to try to follow our intuition, once again to resonate with whatever appears true or real to us.

Todd Ferrier teaches that we are all on a return journey; that we were once beautiful souls in spirit but billions of years ago we made disastrous choices that led to our planet falling into the materialistic wasteland that it is today. We can change it but it will take time.

Before the Fall, Judah, who the Greeks renamed Demeter, lay at the heart of our opaque planet, for then there were no shadows or darkness of any kind. Demeter reflected the divine sunlight and energy and we all supped on the boundless life force of our beautiful goddess, whether we be a flower, unicorn or budding human soul. But in time the warped minds of the fallen angels gradually eclipsed Demeter's shining light until she eventually fell like a stone to the bottom of a deep well, alive but now a prisoner to the obdurate minds of her captors. Today she is gradually recovering her equilibrium as her earth children slowly rise in consciousness.

Demeter stirs as our planet swims
towards the extraordinary equinoctial currents.
As she awakens from her winter somnolence
she receives those solar rays
that have taken just eight minutes to reach her
from the chromosphere of the sun.

With this fertile light Demeter activates nature
with her stunning miracle of autotrophy,
bringing alive vast fields of crops,
commanding her trees to bud and blossom.
Then in autumn her grains are gathered by weary men
and with her harvests now complete she falls asleep again.

Perhaps she will dream of Poseidon
who pursued her when guised as a mare.
Maybe she will create new flowers,
our goddess with golden hair.
Or will she recall her role as a deity
when our planet was still a sublime celestial sphere?

Acknowledgements

I WOULD LIKE to express my gratitude to some of the people who have played such an important role in my 'Fool's Journey'. Especially much love and appreciation to my parents Irene and Fred, who allowed me so much individual freedom to develop as a child/youth. Thanks also to Carol and Kira for their considerable help on this project and not forgetting my grandparents for their past love and support.

I salute the carers at Somertrees OPH circa 1974/6 for their kindness and good-natured humour and especially for the dear old folk passing on through. Thank you to the anonymous 'angel' who somehow encouraged me to become a teacher. Namaste to Antony Bates, my spiritual teacher, who for twenty-five years taught me the ancient esoteric mystery teachings with such aplomb.

Many thanks to Andrew Walpole for his advice and encouragement and finally, a huge thank you to all the kind souls who gave me permission to regurgitate their spiritual stories: Jan M, Tina Cruise, Geoff Stuttaford, Coral Temple, Simon, Ina, Mike Wright, Janis White and my mum!

Notes

1. Jimi Hendrix at the Bromley Court Hotel, 8th February 1967
2. Crystal Palace Garden Party, 15th May 1971
3. Train analogy – early influence by Gurdjieff
4. Finches of Forest Hill (furniture store) – Now Finches Ski Emporium, owned by my good friends Frank and Angela
5. The Order of The Cross, still functioning but without its Kensington headquarters
6. Antony Bates (RIP: 1920-1996): artist, author of *Children of Fire* and *The Dark House*, co-founder of 'The Followers of the Way.'
7. John Todd Ferrier, describes spiritual definitions of Jewish place names (*The Logia*, pages 15 &191)
8. John Todd Ferrier, on the Master's real name (*The Logia*, page 93)
9. John Todd Ferrier, on creation of souls (*Herald 4*, pages 286 & 361; *Life Mysteries Unfolded*, page 168)
10. John Todd Ferrier, explaining the extraordinary Luna (Moon) story of rescuing our planet during

the Fall from Spirit into matter: (*Herald 4*, page 152; *Life Mysteries Unfolded*, page 171)

11. Charlight Utang/Charles Gibaut Bissell-Thomas/Jungleyes Love (RIP: 13.3.56 – 2.2.2013)

12. Bretton Hall Teachers' Training College circa 1974-77

13. This is a quote by Todd Ferrier describing the soul (Extract from *Herald 1*, page 148)

14. Ifield School, Kent, circa 1977-79

15. The Vale School, Haringey circa 1979-1986

16. *The Primal Scream* by Paul Janov (Abacus Books)

17. Married Carol Marples on 28th July 1984 at Norbiton Registry Office

18. Joanna Kira Kemble, daughter, born 14th January 1986

19. Terry Donaldson taught me Tarot at his 'The London Tarot Centre' in 1991. He sadly died aged 58 on 2nd October 2014. RIP

20. Marquardt Middle School, 1912 Glen Ellyn Rd, Glendale Heights, IL 60139, USA circa 1992/93

21. *Grandmother's Secret* by Richard Kemble, 'New Spirals' series, Nelson Thorne 2001

22. Harry Edwards Healing Sanctuary, Burrows Lea Country House, Hook Lane, Shere GU5 9QG

23. Psychic surgeon Stephen Turoff, at Miami Motel, Princes Road, Chelmsford CM2 9AJ

24. *Links of My Life* by Michael Wright (page 15/16)

25. There are at least three myths relating to Mary Magdalene. The first being the familiar New

Testament concoction by the writers of the gospels, whereby Mary faithfully stood by Jesus after his crucifixion and witnessed, sort of, evidence of his resurrection. This story draws heavily upon the Isis myth, for Isis resurrected her dead brother/husband and later bore him a son. The second myth assumes a physical relationship between Jesus and Mary Magdalene with Jesus being humanised as a Jewish man, who had normal desires and duly gave Mary Magdalene a son(s). There are many books that investigate this theme including: *The Meaning of Mary Magdalene* by Cynthia Bourgeault, plus being the plot of a film: *The Da Vinci Code.* Todd Ferrier states that the 'Magdalene' is *not* a person at all but a lowly state of being whereby the soul had abandoned its faith in the divine. This mystery is revealed by Todd Ferrier as part of the 'Oblation' or sin-offering whereby 'Jesus' had forty lives/incarnations in the spiritual wilderness of this world after his beautiful Christhood manifestation. (There are many references to the Oblation in Mr Ferrier's books, including *The Logia* page 163. This sin-offering work was the absorption and transmutation of the evil elemental forms in our spiritual heavens. In his first sin-offering life he lived as a harlot, 'Mercedes' in Nero's Court. Hence the connection to being a Magdalene. (Reference *Herald 16* page 279)

26. Mary Bligh-Bond: *Poems, Visions and Essays*, published by House of John
27. From *Spectrum of Consciousness* by Ken Wilber
28. 'Centaurs – the Hells Angels of mythology' comment attributed to astrologer Dave Arner
29. John Todd Ferrier, on the feeding of the multitude (*The Master*, page 275)
30. John Todd Ferrier, explaining the mystery of 'the two small fishes' (*Herald 4*, page191)
31. John Todd Ferrier, human souls not just on Earth (*Herald 4*, page 276)
32. John Todd Ferrier, no new souls have been made since the Fall (*Herald 4*, page 276)
33. After the ice age, Luna rescued the Earth which had lost all its atmosphere. Sadly, Luna came too close and all its magnetic atmosphere was taken by our planet including its oceans and peoples. Todd Ferrier (*Herald 3*, page 346)
34. Todd Ferrier writes that the Fall of our planet from spirit into matter had a dire effect on all the planets in our solar system. Venus lost its outermost planes and its children were drawn to Earth (*Herald1*, page 345; *Herald 4*, page 191)
35. John Todd Ferrier, on the twelve houses of Judah (*Herald 3*, page 276)
36. John Todd Ferrier, reveals how a minor god led to the fall of our planet into fixity (*Isaiah*, page 155; *Herald 24*, page 83)
37. John Todd Ferrier, on the Lemurians (*Herald 1*, page 344)

38. Hippocrates of Kos, (460 – 370 BC)
39. Barbara Ann Brennan (*Hands of light*, page 148)
40. John Todd Ferrier, on the veils of blood (*Herald 3*, page 359)

A Song for Demeter

An autobiography, incorporating youthful anecdotes,
spiritual visions, earthly conversations, allegorical
stories and astonshing celestial revelations.

Cover painting by Antony Bates
('Jesus born where the creatures are sheltered.')